HEALTH ISSUES

CANCER

Kirsten Lamb

HODDER Wayland

an imprint of Hodder Children's Books

White-Thomson Publishing Ltd,
2-3 St Andrew's Place, Lewes,
East Sussex BN7 1UP

Published in Great Britain in 2002 by Hodder Wayland, an imprint of Hodder Children's Books.

This book was produced for White-Thomson Publishing Ltd by Ruth Nason.

Design: Carole Binding
Picture research: Glass Onion Pictures

British Library Cataloguing in Publication Data
Lamb, Kirsten
Cancer. - (Health issues)
1. Cancer - Juvenile literature
I. Title II. Nason, Ruth
616.9'94

ISBN 0 7502 3945 X

Printed in Hong Kong by Wing King Tong

Hodder Children's Books
A division of Hodder Headline Limited
338 Euston Road, London NW1 3BH

Acknowledgements
The author and publishers thank the following for their permission to reproduce photographs and illustrations: Martyn Chillmaid: pages 44, 48b; Corbis Images: page 9; Angela Hampton Family Life Picture Library: pages 3, 17, 20, 25, 29, 35t, 35rc, 35bl, 35br, 37, 49, 55, 57; Imaging Body: page 42; Impact Photos: pages 10 (Peter Arkell), 43r (John Cole), 54 (Giles Barnard); Mediscan: cover and pages 1 and 53, pages 13, 34, 35lc, 39b; Photofusion: page 4 (Ute Klaphake); Popperfoto/Reuters: pages 11, 24, 32; Science Photo Library: pages 5 (CAMR/A. B. Dowsett), 6 (Dr P. Marazzi), 21 (Simon Fraser), 22 (Kevin Beebe, Custom Medical Stock Photo), 23 (Chris Bjornberg), 26 (BSIP Edwige), 27 (Simon Fraser), 28 (Prof. Aaron Polliack), 36 (Tim Beddow), 39t (Simon Fraser/Royal Victoria Infirmary, Newcastle), 40t (Dr Yorgos Nikas), 40b (Colin Cuthbert), 43l (Doug Plummer), 51 (Simon Fraser), 52 (Colin Cuthbert); Still Pictures: pages 14 (Jorgen Schytte), 19 (Mark Edwards), 31 (Mark Edwards); Topham Picturepoint: page 15. The illustrations on pages 25b and 33 and the photo on page 48t are from the Wayland Picture Library. All other illustrations are by Carole Binding. Information for graphs and illustrations on pages 15, 18, 19 and 30 is reproduced courtesy of the Cancer Research Campaign.

Note: Photographs illustrating the case studies in this book were posed by models.

Contents

1 Cancer and its causes

Cells and why they change

The majority of us will come face to face with cancer at some stage in our lives. Cancer is common. Most of us can think of someone we know, or someone famous, who has experienced the reality of cancer – its diagnosis; treatments; in some cases complete cure; recurrence of the cancer; and possibly death from cancer.

The 'big C': most people are afraid of cancer, worried about being told that they have it, frightened of the effects of cancer treatment, and terrified that they will die from the disease. Many people worry that any symptoms they have inevitably mean cancer – be they skin moles, lumps, chest problems, headaches or bowel troubles. At the same time, many people, knowingly or not, choose a lifestyle that exposes them to risks of cancer. They may be smokers, or lie in the sun in the heat of the day and not worry about burning, or ignore safety instructions for handling dangerous substances. We are all different.

Young people

Cancer is unusual in young people and, by following a healthy lifestyle now, you can reduce your risk of some cancers.

This book aims to give a realistic picture of cancer. It investigates what cancer is, what causes it, and how the occurrence of cancer varies around the world. It provides full facts about the common cancers – their symptoms, diagnosis, treatment and hopes for future treatments. There is practical advice about reducing your risk of cancer, and finally, the book explores how you live as a family when someone has cancer.

So what is cancer?

'Cancer' is the Latin word for 'crab' and describes the creeping movements of cancer cells around the body.

All human beings start life as a single cell. That cell has a cell wall surrounding a jelly-like substance called cytoplasm, within which is the nucleus. The nucleus is sometimes described as the 'brain' of the cell; it contains most of our genetic material in the form of DNA. There is also genetic material in tiny particles in the cytoplasm, called mitochondria. Mitochondria are probably responsible for energy production in the cell, by the reaction between sugar and oxygen.

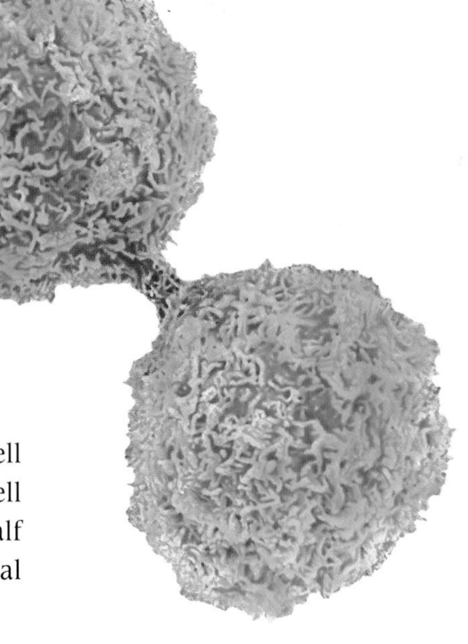

Cell division
This coloured electron micrograph shows a cell dividing to make two new cells.

The first cell divides to make two cells, and this cell division will continue many millions of times. In cell division, the genetic material in the nucleus divides in half and then replicates itself so that the same genetic material is created in each new cell.

As the process continues, the cells start to specialize to become brain cells, skin cells, gut cells, blood cells and so on. There are over 200 cell types in the human body. Under the control of the nucleus, each cell has specific functions and a specific life span. Most of our body is constantly regenerating and repairing itself. For example, hair grows, and skin cells grow across wounds. But the system stays in control. Each individual cell is programmed to die and to be replaced by others.

When cancer occurs, that control mechanism is lost. Cells continue to multiply indefinitely, producing an ever-larger mass of cancer cells. This mass then spreads and invades healthy tissue around it. As it spreads, it can invade blood vessels and lymphatic vessels and be transported to other parts of the body where the process continues. There are over 200 cell types in the body and so there are over 200 types of cancer.

Melanoma
A melanoma is a skin cancer involving pigmented cells.

Think of a skin cell in a mole, for example. Something happens to the DNA in its nucleus and the cell loses its programme to die at the right time and starts to multiply in an uncontrolled way. The mole becomes bigger and darker and may bleed. The abnormal cells spread in the lymphatic system (see page 7) to the local lymph glands. These swell to make lumps. The cancer cells also enter the bloodstream and are deposited all round the body. Skin cancer cells grow in the liver, brain and lungs. Eventually, without treatment, the abnormal cells take over most of the organs of the body and the person cannot survive.

Cancer definitions

- *A mass of cancer cells is commonly called a **tumour**.*
- *Not all cancers are solid masses. Cancers of blood cells (for example, leukaemia) are abnormal cells increasing rapidly and circulating in the bloodstream.*
- *Cells dividing out of control and having the capacity to spread from where they start are called **malignant**. Cancers are malignant tumours.*
- *Lumps of tissue in the body that have no capacity to increase and multiply out of control are called **benign** tumours. They are NOT cancers.*

What causes the change in a cell's DNA? – i.e. what causes cancer?

This is the million-dollar question and the subject of much medical research all around the world for many years. The answer, as with most things in life, is not simple and not fully understood. A normal cell's behaviour is programmed within that cell's DNA. Whenever cells divide and multiply there is a chance that things may go wrong – that the replicating DNA may be altered or 'mutate'. The normal cell carries genes that try to control that. They are DNA repair genes, oncogenes that accelerate growth, and tumour suppressor genes that slow down growth. For cancer to happen, it seems that the cell's DNA is damaged and then a series of mutations occur which end up releasing the cell from its normal control mechanisms. From present evidence, it seems that the oncogenes, tumour suppressor genes and DNA repair genes are very important in this process. The mutations in DNA can be inherited or can be acquired during life.

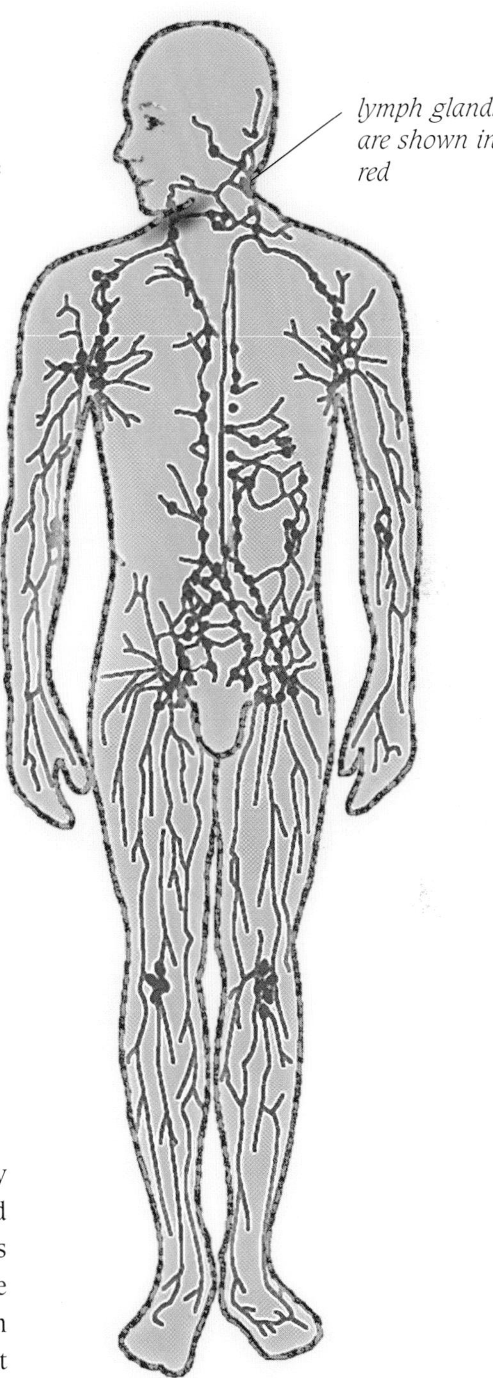

The lymphatic system
This is a system of vessels that carry fluid from around cells back to the bloodstream. Its function is to remove toxic substances.

Inherited cancer risk

At present, we are uncertain how many cancers have a genetic or inherited component. In some families some cancers occur commonly. For example, there are families in which virtually all the women suffer from breast cancer during their adult lives. In some of these families abnormal genes have been discovered. These are known as BRCA1 and BRCA2 genes. Women who carry either of these genes have a much increased chance of getting breast cancer.

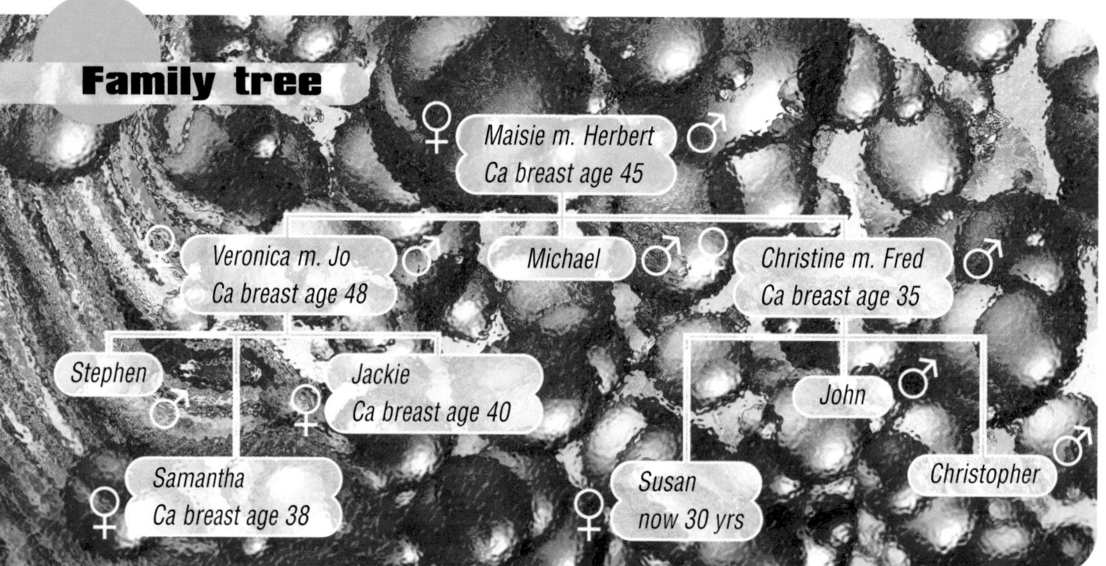

Breast cancer
Maisie's family is one in which the women carry a gene that increases their risk of developing breast cancer. ('Ca' stands for 'cancer'.)

It is thought that the gene is involved with loss of DNA repair. However, only 5 per cent of breast cancer cases are inherited in this way.

Some types of bowel cancer are also inherited. The genes responsible for these cancers running in families have not been identified. Some families show a high frequency of a condition called familial polyposis coli – where little growths or polyps occur in the bowel. These have a high chance of becoming cancerous growths. It is thought that there is a gene abnormality on the fifth chromosome in these families. Another type of bowel cancer that is more common in certain families is called hereditary non-polyposis colorectal cancer. Only one per cent of all cancers of the bowel are in these inherited categories.

There are other families in which different types of cancer cluster, such as cancers of the uterus, ovaries or urinary tract. An abnormal gene concerned with the repair of faulty DNA has been found in these families. However, most cancer is *not* inherited. Most cancers occur because of an assault on the cell's DNA during a person's life. As our body's defence mechanisms age, cancer becomes more common.

Carcinogens – DNA's attackers

Things that attack DNA and so cause cancer are called 'carcinogens'. They include chemicals and radiation.

Chemicals

Worldwide, there are over 50,000 chemicals in production – drugs, plastics, fertilizers, pesticides, and so on. Chemicals were first recognized as causing cancer in 1775. A British surgeon, Sir Percival Pott, noticed that a cancer of the skin of the scrotum was common in young men working as chimney sweeps, and the carbon deposits in soot were found to be responsible. Yet it was not until the early twentieth century that the effect was confirmed by animal testing. Many hydrocarbons and tars cause cancer. The most familiar is the tar in cigarette smoke. The link between smoking and *lung* cancer was established by the pioneering work of Sir Richard Doll in the UK in the 1950s, but it is now thought that 33 per cent of *all* cancers are linked to smoking.

Danger at work
For chimney sweeps, contact with carbon in soot caused cancer.

Methods of study

__Epidemiology__ and __cellular biology__ are two ways in which scientists try to work out what causes cancer.

- *Epidemiologists study the frequency of cancers in different populations and try to establish a link between each cancer and a specific carcinogen to which people have been exposed.*
- *Cellular biologists grow cells from mammals in the laboratory and then observe the DNA mutations caused by adding substances that may be carcinogenic. They may also use animals, including genetically altered mice, to study whether potential carcinogens cause specific cancers.*

Many other chemicals are now known to be carcinogenic. They include some that are present in the environment. However, the amounts of these environmental chemicals to which populations are exposed are too small to cause damage. For example, burning waste produces toxic poisons in the atmosphere, such as dioxins, and these are known to be carcinogenic. But the levels to which communities are exposed are too small to cause cancer in individuals. Clearly, in order to prevent cancer, chemical carcinogens in the environment should be monitored and controlled.

Chemical carcinogens

- *Tar in cigarette smoke → lung cancer and others*
- *Aniline dyes used in the rubber industry for softening rubber → bladder cancer*
- *Asbestos used for lagging pipes → a rare form of lung cancer called mesothelioma*

Radiation

Some frequencies of electromagnetic radiation are known to be carcinogenic, including X-rays and ultraviolet radiation, for example, in sunlight.

Wilhelm Konrad Röntgen discovered X-rays in 1895 and Marie Curie discovered the radioactive substance radium in 1896. It was noticed in the early twentieth century that people working with X-rays were more likely than others to acquire a range of cancers, from skin cancers to the blood cancer, leukaemia. The effects of radiation were studied further after two devastating incidents: the dropping of atomic bombs on Hiroshima and Nagasaki in Japan at the end of the Second World War in 1945, and the accident at the nuclear power station at Chernobyl, Ukraine, in 1986.

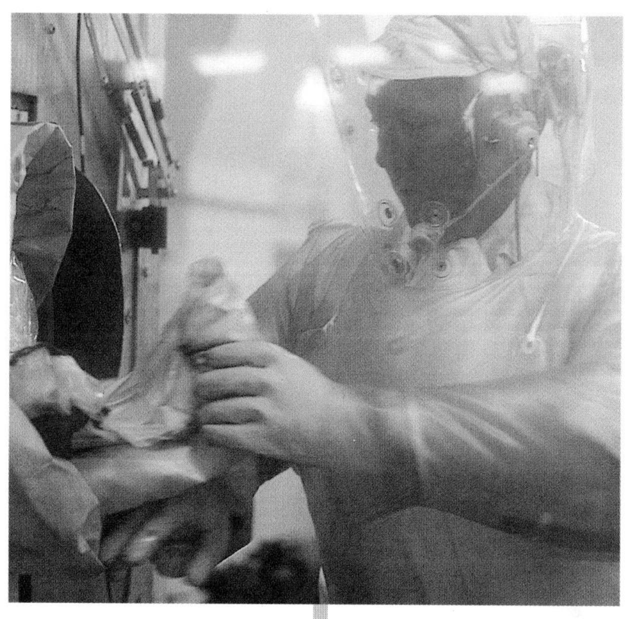

Protection at work
A worker at an atomic research centre wears fully protective clothing.

The populations of Hiroshima and Nagasaki have been closely monitored since 1945. In the first ten years the incidence of leukaemia in the population was far higher than normal. Thirty years on, the incidence of solid tumours increased markedly.

'My grandmother and her sisters were teenagers when the bomb was dropped on Hiroshima. Her younger sister died of leukaemia five years later. Her older sister developed breast cancer in her forties. We don't need to learn about the bombs at school – we hear about their effects in our families.'
(Maki, age 15)

The accident at Chernobyl released 200 times the amount of radiation of the Hiroshima and Nagasaki bombs combined. One of the first radioactive substances released was radioactive iodine. This was rapidly absorbed by the thyroid glands of people living in the area. Iodine is used by the thyroid in the production of hormone. Five years later the incidence of thyroid cancer soared. It is normally rare. The cancer was commonest in children, particularly those under five when they were exposed to radiation.

After Chernobyl
A father feeds his children at a special hospital in Belarus, dealing with radiation-related illnesses.

Lower-frequency radiation

X-rays and ultraviolet (UV) radiation are both high-frequency, short-wave-length radiation in the electromagnetic spectrum. This spectrum ranges from X-rays and UV down through visible light to low-frequency infrared, microwaves and radio waves. There is no evidence that radiation with a frequency below UV radiation is carcinogenic. Common sources of such radiation are mobile phones and microwave cookers. There is also no evidence that electric and magnetic fields (for example, around high-voltage electricity pylons) cause cancer.

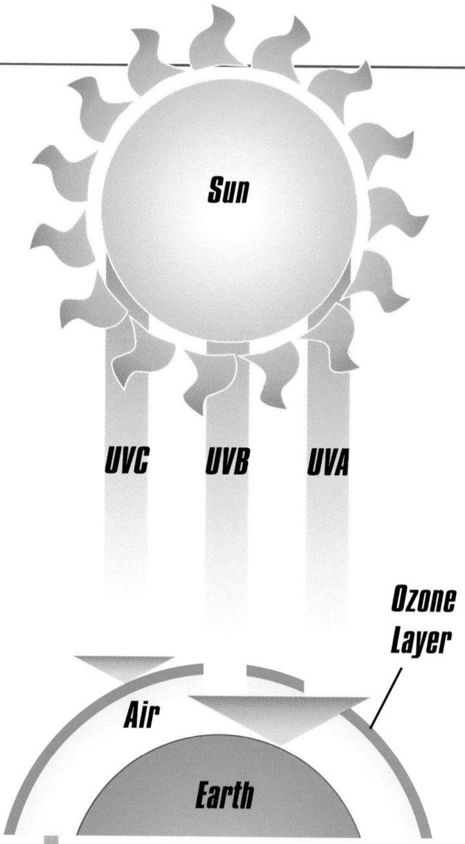

Ultraviolet radiation

Ultraviolet (UV) radiation from the sun is a well-recognized cause of skin cancer. This type of radiation is also produced artificially in sun lamps used to induce tanning. UV radiation is electromagnetic radiation of different wavelengths. It is divided into UVA, UVB and UVC. Most is in the UVA range and causes darkening of a pigment in the skin (i.e. tanning). It does not burn the skin, but does cause damage to deeper layers. UVB is of shorter wavelength and *does* burn the skin. Most UVC radiation from the sun, the shortest wavelength, is blocked by the ozone layer around the earth. UVC is extremely damaging to the skin.

Studies by epidemiologists show there are more cases of skin cancer in people who are exposed most to sunlight. Skin pigmentation protects the skin, so white populations living in countries with high UV radiation exposure – such as Australia and South Africa – have a high incidence of all skin cancers.

Solar UV radiation
UVA and UVB radiation pass through the ozone layer to reach the earth. The more harmful UVC is blocked by the ozone layer.

Infections – viruses and bacteria

It is thought that viruses may be involved in 15 per cent of cancers worldwide. Viruses consist of genetic material (DNA or RNA) surrounded by a protein coat. They invade the DNA of a cell and then use the cell's mechanisms to multiply. This direct action on a cell's DNA is probably how viruses can, in some circumstances, produce the mutations that allow the cell to become a cancer cell.

In 1910 it was discovered that a virus could cause cancer in chickens. The first virus found to cause a human cancer is known as HTLV1. In the 1970s scientists noticed that in fishing villages in South Japan many more people than normal suffered from lymphomas (cancers of the lymph glands) and leukaemia. A very similar virus to HTLV1 was found in the cells of these cancers.

Human papilloma virus (HPV), a sexually transmitted infection, is thought to be the cause of most cases of cancer of the cervix. Two types of the virus, HPV 16 and 18, are found in 80 per cent of tissue samples from tumours of the cervix. Testing for these viruses may become part of cervical cancer screening (see page 51).

The hepatitis B virus causes infection of the liver and is widespread in Africa. In the same part of the world, liver cancer is also very common. The hepatitis B virus is found in cancer cells in the liver and it is therefore assumed that the virus helps cause liver cancer.

There is as yet little evidence that bacteria are involved in cancer formation. However, recently, it has been noticed that a bacterium found in the stomach and often associated with stomach ulcers is also found much more frequently in people with stomach cancer. The bacterium is called Helicobacter pylori.

As you can see, cancer is complex. We do not know the causes of all cancers. Probably many are the result of a mixture of inherited risk and assault on our cells by a variety of agents.

Burkitt's lymphoma

These tumours of lymph glands were found to be common in children in parts of Africa.

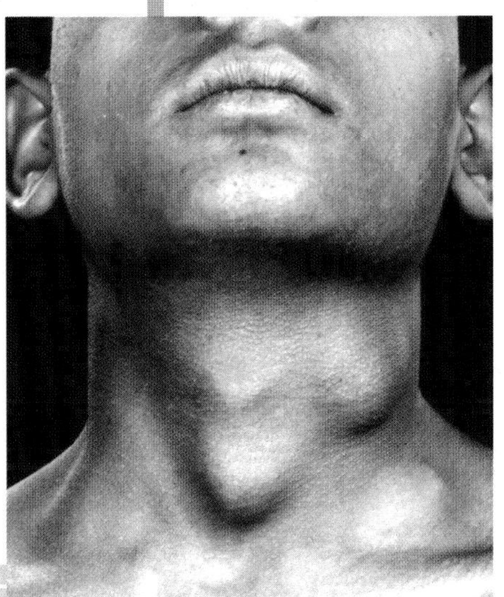

Burkitt's lymphoma

*While working as a surgeon in Uganda in the 1960s, Dennis Burkitt noticed that a type of lymphoma was particularly common in children. A virus known as the Epstein-Barr virus was found in the tumour tissue. Interestingly, this is the same virus that causes glandular fever – an infection (**not** a tumour) of lymph glands that is common in the Western world. Burkitt's lymphoma is very uncommon in the West, and glandular fever is uncommon in the parts of Africa with a high rate of Burkitt's lymphoma. It is thought that circumstances cause the Epstein-Barr virus to produce the mutations that lead to cancer. These circumstances probably include malnutrition and malaria infection.*

2 Cancer around the world
How and why it varies

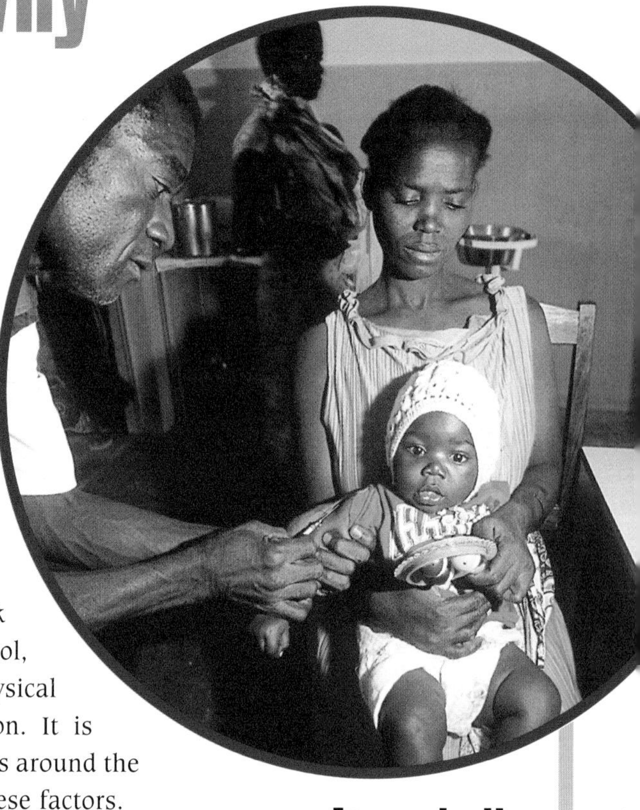

In the year 2000 there were an estimated 10.3 million new cases of cancer worldwide. The types of cancer that are commonest vary between countries and between parts of the same country. These variations are very obvious and support the idea that cancer is caused by carcinogens to which populations are exposed. Around the world, the main causes of cancer, or risk factors for it, are tobacco, diet, alcohol, infection, sexual behaviour and geophysical factors such as sunlight and radiation. It is possible that up to 80 per cent of cancers around the world are preventable by controlling these factors.

Immunization
Immunizing children in Africa against hepatitis B helps to reduce their risk of liver cancer.

So how does cancer vary around the world?

Half the new cases of cancer occur in the developed world and half in the developing world. Across the world, lung cancer is the most common cancer. In the developed world this is followed by bowel cancer and breast cancer. But in parts of Africa, liver cancer is by far the most common cancer. Reasons for this are thought to be high rates of infection with the hepatitis B virus (see page 13) and also the contamination of food with a toxin called aflatoxin. Aflatoxin comes from a mould that appears on nuts and cereals that are not stored properly. Both the hepatitis B virus and aflatoxin are thought to be carcinogenic to the liver. To try to improve the situation, children in Africa are being immunized against hepatitis B.

Stomach cancer and diet

It is thought that the Japanese diet, consisting of large amounts of smoked and salted fish, might contribute to the country's high incidence of stomach cancer.

Stomach cancer is the commonest cancer in Japan, but generally around the world cancer of the stomach is becoming less common. There is a suspicion that most stomach cancer is linked to diet. The way that food is preserved has changed dramatically. In the past, before refrigeration, food was preserved by smoking it or salting it. A diet of mostly salted or smoked food probably increases the risk of stomach cancer.

The developed world

One person in three in the developed world will have cancer at some stage in their life. Cancer is commoner the older you get – so 65 per cent of people over 65 years old will develop a cancer. The common cancers in Europe and

Incidence of cancers in the UK (1997)

Lung cancer	38,870
Breast cancer	38,270
Colorectal cancer	34,310
Prostate cancer	21,770
Bladder cancer	12,730
Stomach cancer	10,480
Leukaemia	6,160
Melanoma	5,710
Cancer of the uterus	4,850

the USA are lung cancer, breast cancer and 'colorectal' or bowel cancer. About half of all cancers are one of these three. Leukaemia is the commonest cancer in children, representing one third of all childhood cancers. Cancer of the testicle is the commonest cancer in men aged 20-39.

Important stats

- 25 per cent of all deaths in the UK and USA are caused by cancer.
- In the UK cancer is the biggest killer.
- 25 per cent of all cancer deaths worldwide are from lung cancer.
- 90 per cent of all lung cancer deaths in the world are linked to smoking.
- 33 per cent of all cancer deaths in the world are linked to smoking.

Cancer and smoking

It is thought that around 30 per cent of all cancers around the world are caused by smoking. Most types of lung cancer are directly caused by smoking and many other types of cancer also have smoking as a significant cause. These are cancers of the lip, tongue, mouth, larynx or voice box, pharynx or back of the mouth, bladder, pancreas, oesophagus, stomach, kidney and cervix, and also leukaemia.

Changes over time

These graphs show how the rates of deaths from different cancers have changed over time.

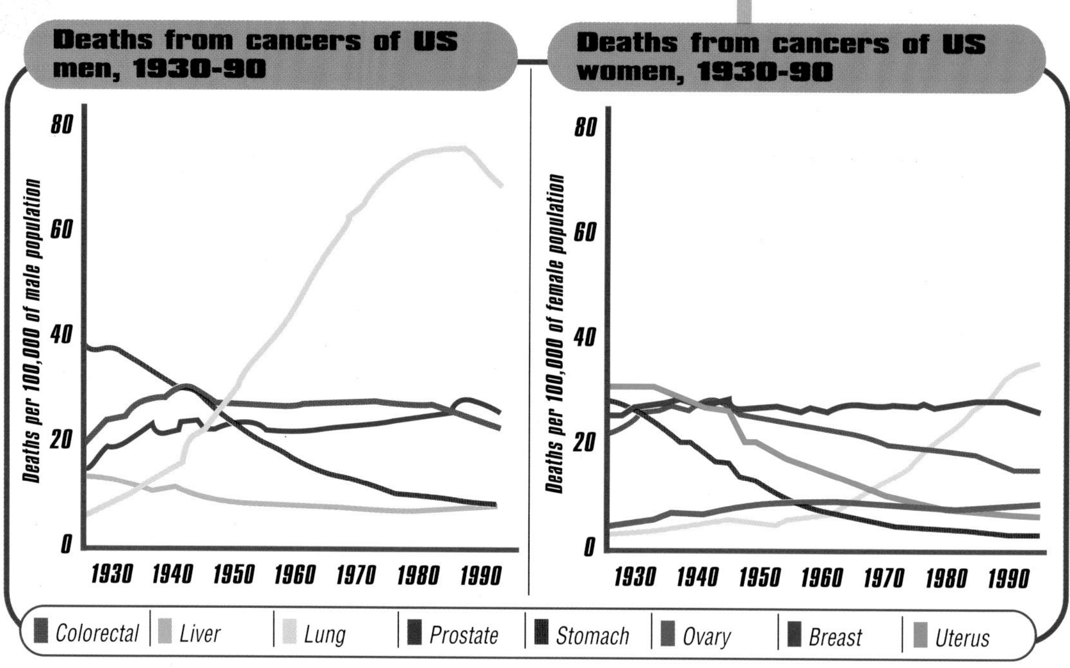

As patterns of smoking behaviour change, corresponding changes occur in the incidence of cancers caused by smoking. Patterns of lung cancer follow the patterns of smoking. In the early twentieth century lung cancer was rare. In the UK and the USA, the death rate from lung cancer in men peaked in the 1980s, but it is still rising in women. This reflects the fact that male smoking reached a peak in the late 1940s, whereas women took up smoking more and more until the 1970s. There is a time lag between the start of smoking and developing lung cancer.

Smoking through the generations

Caitlin's great-great-grandfather Albert was born at the beginning of the twentieth century. When he was young, smoking was becoming popular amongst men his age, but he despised any woman who smoked, and not many did.

Albert's son John fought in the Second World War. By the end of the war almost all men of his age smoked about 20 cigarettes a day. A few of the women he knew had started to smoke, but he liked his wife, Ann, to be a non-smoker.

John's and Ann's children, Peter and Mary, were teenagers in the 1950s and enjoyed the rock and roll era. Peter's son Richard was born in 1965. It was while Richard and his wife-to-be, Joanna, were teenagers that girls and women started to become regular smokers. Richard and Joanna smoked together when they went out. But they were aware that smoking damages your health and they managed to give up. In fact, by the time Caitlin was born in 1988, most of her parents' generation had stopped smoking.

Caitlin and her friends have all started smoking. They don't see that it is any problem to them. They know it is bad for them, but all feel confident that they will stop. Their parents are concerned because they know it won't be that easy.

Caitlin
The story of Caitlin's family shows how smoking behaviour has changed over time.

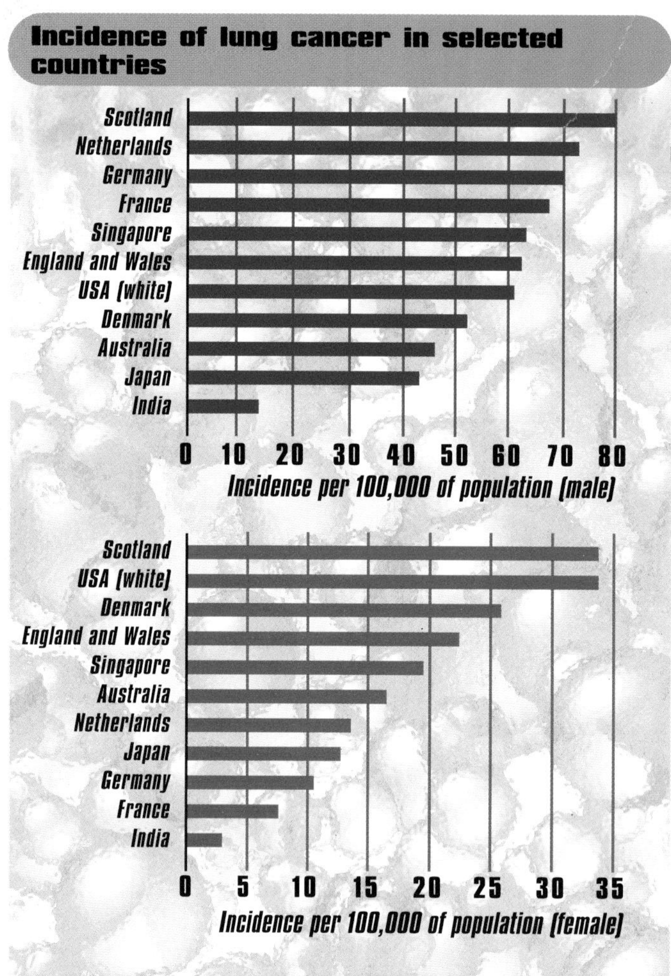

Lung cancer
These graphs show how the incidence of lung cancer differs between men and women in different countries.

As fewer people in the developed world smoke, the tobacco companies market their product aggressively in developing countries. As more people in these countries take up smoking, so there is a rise in lung cancer there and in the death rates from the disease. Now, in China, an estimated 70 per cent of men over 25 are smoking – some 300 million people. An epidemic of lung cancer will follow. It is estimated that by the year 2020 tobacco-related deaths may rise to 7 million per year in the developing world.

Fact

Take 1,000 20-year-olds. One will die from murder or manslaughter and six in road accidents. But, if the 1,000 are all smokers, 250 will die from smoking-related disease in middle age.

It is not just the smokers themselves that we must worry about. It is thought that one quarter of all lung cancers in non-smokers are caused by passive smoking – that is, breathing in the smoke from somebody else's cigarette.

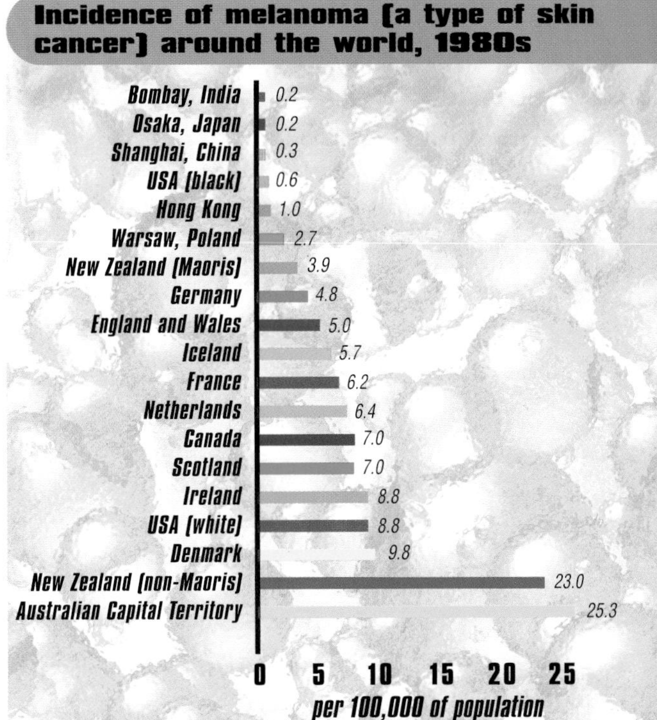

Skin cancers

Skin cancers are strongly associated with exposure to sunlight. There are wide variations in skin cancer rates around the world. People at greatest risk are those with fair skin, blue eyes, freckles, many moles and who burn easily. People with pigmented skin have much greater protection against skin cancer. It is ultraviolet radiation from sunlight that is the problem. Exposure to UV radiation is greater, the closer you are to the equator and the higher your altitude. It is also increased by reflection from snow, sand and water. A striking contrast is seen between Maoris and non-Maoris in New Zealand. The fairer-skinned non-Maoris have a much higher rate of melanoma.

In the outback

Dan is 18. He was born and brought up in Australia, in the outback. 'When I was a little kid we just used to play outside around the farm, naked. Nobody was worried. My brother and I often got burnt. It was kind of fun at night to peel the burnt and blistering skin off each other's backs. Now we are paranoid. I surf and play cricket. I'm really careful now. There are patrols on the beach telling people to cream up and to wear their hats. It's better to barbie in the evening when the sun isn't so powerful. I just hope it's not too late for me.'

3 Common cancers
Their effects and diagnosis

A lifetime smoker
Frank must face the fact that death rates from lung cancer are high.

Frank talks about lung cancer

Caroline's grandfather Frank says: 'I've smoked all my life. I tried to stop in my late 20s, but everyone else was still smoking so what was the point? I'm 65 now and have just been diagnosed with lung cancer. I went to the doctor first before Christmas. I was coughing up green phlegm and felt ill. The doctor gave me some antibiotics. I got a bit better but by the end of January I had started coughing up some blood. The doctor knew I was a smoker so he arranged a chest X-ray. He called me in to see him after that and said the X-ray showed a shadow in my right lung. I feared the worst. He said I needed some further tests and sent me to a chest surgeon who arranged a bronchoscopy. I had an anaesthetic and a tube was passed down my throat into my lungs. A piece of tissue from the area with the shadow was taken and sent to the laboratory to be investigated under the microscope. This is called taking a biopsy. The biopsy proved that I have lung cancer. The surgeon saw me to tell me all this and to discuss what we should do next. He was very honest with me and told me what my chances of survival are and what choices I have about treatment.'

! The Facts

Lung cancer

- Most types of lung cancer start in the cells that line the bronchi – the main tubes into the lungs.
- Worldwide it is the commonest cancer. The incidence in men has started to fall as male smoking reduces. The incidence in women is still rising. Lung cancer is commoner when you are over 40.

- Survival rates are generally poor for people with lung cancer, as it is rarely found before it has started to spread around the body. In the USA in 1995, only 14 per cent of people with lung cancer survived for five years. For lung cancers found early and before they spread, 42 per cent of people survive for five years.
- The most well-known cause is smoking.
- Early cancers have very few symptoms. Later symptoms are a cough that does not go away; chest pain with deep breathing; blood in phlegm; weight loss and no appetite.
- As the tumour grows, cancer cells can break off and spread to other parts of the body. They spread most commonly to the lymph glands (lumps can be felt in the armpit or neck); the liver (yellow skin colouring called jaundice may develop and the enlarged liver may become uncomfortable); and bone (this causes pain in the ribs or other bones).
- Tests for lung cancer are: a chest X ray; sputum cytology – which looks for cancer cells in phlegm; bronchoscopy and biopsy – taking tissue from the tumour to look at under the microscope; and a CT scan – a computerized X-ray that can look at the organs of the body. It is used to check whether the tumour has spread from the lungs to other parts of the body.
- Treatment by surgery is only possible in 20 per cent of people with lung cancer. The surgeon removes a part or the whole of a lung in order to get rid of the tumour. Radiotherapy (see page 36) is used to shrink the tumour in people who are too ill for surgery, or to attack the tumour when it spreads to bones, to help lessen the bone pain.

X-ray
This coloured X-ray shows the ribcage and lungs. The red-yellow patch is a tumour.

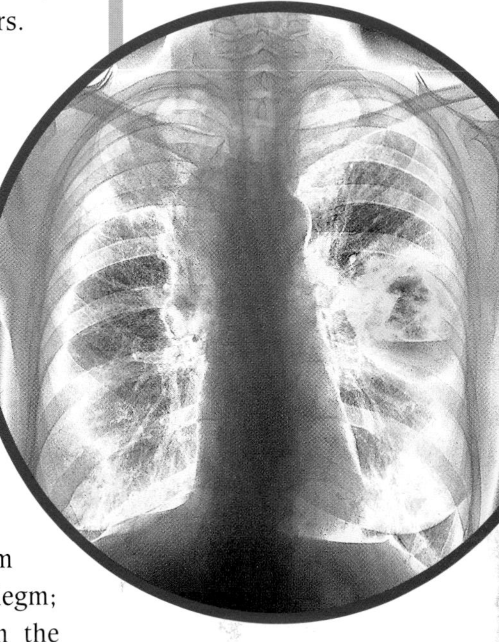

Staging

To decide on treatment for a patient diagnosed with cancer, the cancer is 'staged'. This means that the size of the tumour is measured and any spread to lymph glands and to anywhere else is noted. This is called 'TNM classification'. T is for the tumour size. N is whether lymph glands are involved. M is whether there are metastases – the medical term for spread to other parts of the body.

Margaret learns she has breast cancer

Victoria's mother Margaret is 45 and has just been diagnosed with breast cancer. 'It's been a terrible 2-3 weeks. I was showering after going to the gym and was feeling my breasts and checking them in the mirror. I do that every now and again. When I felt a lump in my left breast, my heart just turned over. My husband was great and got me a doctor's appointment. The doctor examined my breasts and advised me to go to the breast clinic at the local hospital.

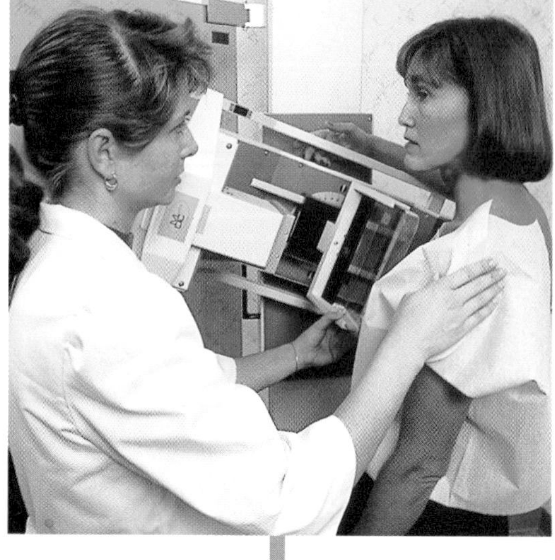

Mammogram
A radiographer shows Margaret how to stand for the X-ray of her breast.

I was terrified, but they were marvellous at the clinic. The specialist talked to me and examined me and then sent me for an X-ray of my breasts called a mammogram. He said he was a little suspicious, so he needed to put a needle into the lump to take some cells to send to the lab. He called it a needle biopsy. I went back 3 days later for the results. I had a long chat with a nurse counsellor, who explained what will happen next. I've got to have a scan to check that the cancer hasn't spread. Then my operation is planned for next week. As the lump is quite small, they are just going to remove it and leave the rest of my breast. When I've recovered from the operation I will have radiotherapy to stop any remaining cancer cells from growing. Then I will take a drug called tamoxifen for 5 years. They tell me this drug blocks the effect of my own body's hormone oestrogen. I feel really positive now and won't let the cancer beat me.'

The Facts

Breast cancer

- Breast cancer starts in the cells that line the tubes and milk-producing glands of the breast.
- It is the commonest cancer in women, although lung cancer kills more women. It is rare under the age of 30. Over a lifetime, a woman has a 1 in 10 risk of having breast cancer.

- Survival rates are increasing as breast cancer is detected earlier and treatment is improved. Survival depends on how far advanced the disease is when it is found. For women who have a small lump, with no spread outside the breast when the cancer is found, 98 per cent survive for five years. For women who are diagnosed with advanced disease, spread to other parts of the body at the time they are first seen, only 16 per cent survive for five years.
- The actual cause of breast cancer is not known, but many things increase or decrease a woman's risk of getting it (see below). Women are at lower risk if they have breast-fed their babies.
- Symptoms of breast cancer that women should look out for are: a lump in the breast; a change in shape of the breast; pulling in of the nipple on one side; dimpling of skin over the breast; discharge of fluid or blood from the nipple.
- Breast cancers spread first to the lymph glands nearest the breast. Lumps may be felt in the armpit. It can then spread in the bloodstream to the liver, brain and bones.

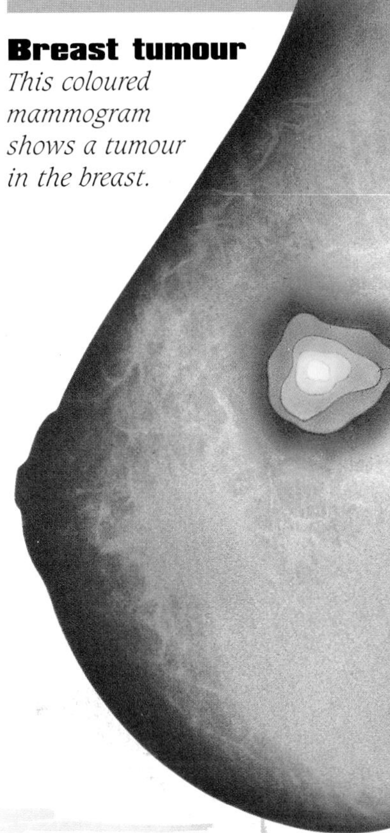

Breast tumour
This coloured mammogram shows a tumour in the breast.

Risk factors for breast cancer

A woman's risk of breast cancer is increased if she:

- carries the BRCA1 or BRCA2 gene (see page 7).

- menstruates for more years than average (starting periods at an early age and ending them, at the menopause, after the age of 50).

- does not have any pregnancies.

- uses the combined oral contraceptive pill for many years (slightly increased risk).

- takes hormone replacement therapy after the menopause (very slightly increased risk).

- drinks alcohol. 2-5 units of alochol per day increases risk by 1.5 times.

- is overweight. It seems that fatty tissue is responsible for making some of the body's hormone oestrogen. Most breast cancers need oestrogen to continue to thrive.

- Tests for breast cancer are a mammogram (breast X-ray) and needle biopsy.
- The cancer is staged (see page 21) to decide on treatment. Sometimes it is possible for the surgeon to simply remove the lump. If the lump is very large, then the whole breast is removed – this is called mastectomy. Nowadays it is often possible for the woman to have the breast reconstructed using an artificial implant. The lymph glands under the arm are also removed at the operation to check whether the tumour has spread to them. Usually, radiotherapy (see page 36) is given after surgery to kill any tumour cells that may have been missed. Chemotherapy (page 38) may also be given to women whose tumour is more advanced, or as an extra safety measure to try to kill tumour cells that may have started to spread.

Campaigners

Some women who survive breast cancer campaign to increase awareness of the disease. American singer Jo Dee Messina led a chorus of such women at a 'Race for the Cure' concert, June 2001.

Tamoxifen

Many breast cancers need the female hormone oestrogen to help their growth. The drug tamoxifen blocks the effect of the body's oestrogen. It is used for 5 years after breast cancer surgery to try to prevent the tumour re-growing.

Alan has treatment for bowel cancer

Alan is 70. 'A couple of years ago I had a bad time. All my life I had been really regular, opening my bowels. I started to notice things were different. I'd go for spells being constipated and then it would be really loose for a period. I didn't take much notice, but then I started passing blood and that was unusual. I'd read in the paper that this was something to look out for in case it was cancer. I went to the doctor and tests were arranged. I had a sigmoidoscopy. They pass a tube up through your back passage and look inside the bowel. They took a sample and found out that there was a cancer in my bowel. I had some other tests including a scan, to check that nothing else was involved, and then I had an operation to remove a segment of my bowel. I've been really lucky because the tumour was caught early and I don't need any other treatment. They say my chances are really good. It was a big shock, though, to have to go through all that.'

The Facts

Bowel cancer

- Bowel (or colon) cancer starts in the cells that line the large bowel – the colon and rectum.
- It spreads through the bowel wall to the neighbouring tissue in the abdomen. Then it can spread to the liver by the bloodstream.
- It is relatively common. It is rare below the age of 40, and 90 per cent of cases occur over the age of 50. The death rate from bowel cancer is falling, partly because it is becoming less common, it is being found earlier and treatment is better.
- 90 per cent of people with an early cancer survive for five years and 65 per cent of those whose cancer has just spread through the wall of the bowel survive for

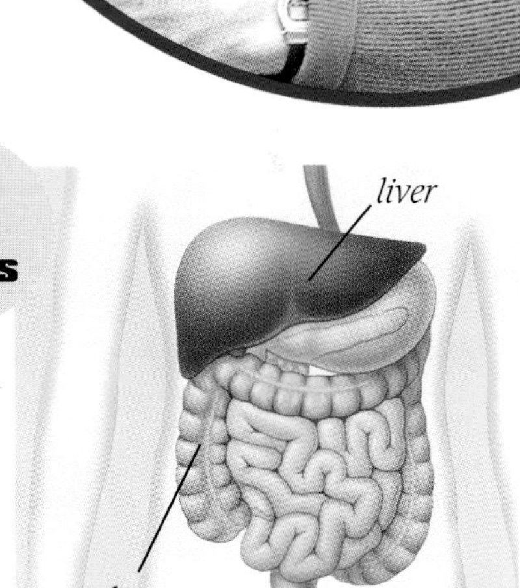

The large bowel
The 'large bowel' consists of the colon and rectum.

Factors that increase the risk of bowel cancer

- Some families carry a gene that increases their risk of bowel cancer (see page 8).
- Polyps (little growths) on the bowel wall can turn into tumours.
- A disease called ulcerative colitis, where the wall of the colon becomes very inflamed, increases the risk of bowel cancer.
- It seems that a diet high in animal fats and low in fibre increases the risk.
- Being overweight, taking no exercise, smoking and high alcohol intake all increase the risk.

five years; but only 8 per cent of people whose cancer has spread further (for example to the liver) survive for five years.

- The cause is not fully understood, but may be related to diet.
- Symptoms of bowel cancer are: a change in bowel habit; feeling that the bowel is not completely empty; passing blood and mucus from the back passage; weight loss and loss of appetite; abdominal pain.
- Sigmoidoscopy is one test for bowel cancer. It means looking inside the bowel by passing a metal tube up through the back passage. Flexible sigmoidoscopy uses a flexible tube, and colonoscopy is a test where a long flexible tube is used to look at the whole length of the colon. Another test is called a barium enema. For this, a white mixture is poured through a tube into the colon and then X-rays are taken. The white mixture shows the outline of the bowel on the X-ray. Tests used to check whether the cancer has spread include ultrasound scan, to look at the liver, CT scan, and chest X-ray.

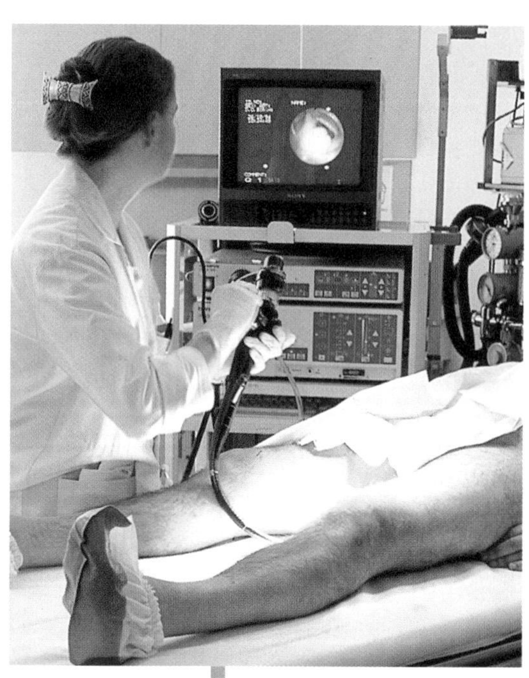

Colonoscopy
A doctor uses a colonoscope to examine a patient's colon. An image of the inside of the colon appears on the screen.

- If the cancer found is very small (i.e. a few cancer cells in a polyp), the surgeon can remove it through a sigmoidoscope. If the cancer is larger, then a section of the bowel needs to be removed. Usually it is possible for the surgeon simply to stitch the remaining two ends of bowel together again. Sometimes this is not possible and the end of the bowel is brought out to the skin; faeces are then passed through this and into a bag – this is called colostomy. Radiotherapy (page 36) is used only occasionally for bowel cancer, if the tumour is too large to remove. Chemotherapy (page 38) is sometimes used in addition to surgery.

Annabelle copes with leukaemia

Annabelle is 10. 'I've just finished having treatment for leukaemia. It's gone on for 3 years and I'm fed up with it. Everyone at the hospital tells me I've done really well. Mum said it all started when I was 7. I was only ill for a couple of weeks. I got very tired and pale. My gums were bleeding when I brushed my teeth and I kept getting bruises. The doctor took a blood test and phoned us the same day to say I must be rushed to hospital. The number of white blood cells in my blood was very high.

I had to have a bone marrow test – a big needle was drilled into the bone above my hip, and cells from inside were looked at. And I had a lumbar puncture – a needle into my back to collect fluid from my spinal canal. Then chemotherapy treatment started – very powerful drugs were injected into my blood. It was very hard at the beginning. I felt really ill and everything got worse. I lost all my hair. I couldn't play with friends because it was very easy for me to catch nasty infections. I cried and cried, but Mum and Dad and the nurses and doctors were always there to help me.'

Annabelle
A nurse makes notes during Annabelle's long treatment.

The Facts

Leukaemia

- Leukaemia is a cancer of white blood cells. It starts in the bone marrow where blood cells are made and spreads to the bloodstream, lymph glands, liver, spleen and other places such as the brain.
- Adults and children can get leukaemia, but it is the commonest cancer in children. Children born with abnormal immune systems have an increased risk of getting leukaemia. Exposure to radiation also increases the risk.
- More than 80 per cent of children survive after treatment for leukaemia. The chances are less good for very young babies and children who get leukaemia over the age of 10.
- Symptoms of leukaemia are related to what is happening in the blood. As white blood cells multiply out of control, fewer red blood cells are made and this causes a condition called anaemia, which makes the child tired and weak. Fewer platelets are made, and this stops the blood clotting properly and therefore causes bruising and bleeding.
- After bone marrow tests and a lumbar puncture, as described by Annabelle (page 27), and scans to show where else in the body is involved, the person is treated with chemotherapy. Powerful drugs that stop cells dividing are injected into the blood. These kill the rapidly multiplying leukaemia cells but also kill other cells that multiply fast, such as hair and other blood cells. During treatment the child is at risk of catching infections, bruising, bleeding and hair loss. Drugs are also injected into the spinal canal. The first phase of treatment is the most aggressive and is called induction. Maintenance treatment is then given. The whole process takes 2-3 years.

Blood cells
In normal blood there are many more red blood cells than white ones. In this coloured electron micrograph the white blood cells are coloured yellow.

Rick has skin cancer

Rick is 25. 'I'm very fair with red hair. When I was a kid I was always getting burnt because I was in and out of the pool and couldn't be bothered with sun creams. Then in my holidays I worked on building sites – always bare-chested. A while ago I noticed that a mole on my shoulder had got bigger and darker and started itching. My Mum said I should go to the doctor, and the doctor sent me to a skin specialist – a dermatologist. He suggested that the mole should be removed. A few days later I had a message asking me to go back to the clinic. I was told that it was a melanoma – a type of skin cancer. I needed to see a plastic surgeon to have a much bigger piece of skin removed from around where the mole had been. Apparently, they measure how thick the mole is, to work out how dangerous it will be and what type of treatment I will need.'

A good outlook

Rick's cancer has been found at an early stage. It should be possible to treat it successfully.

The Facts

Melanoma

- Melanoma starts in melanocytes. These are pigment-making cells in the skin.
- It spreads first to the closest lymph glands. Then it can spread in the bloodstream to almost any part of the body – lungs, liver, brain, etc.
- Melanoma is the cancer whose incidence is increasing most rapidly. Worldwide, the number of new cases has doubled in the last 15 years. It is the third most common cancer in women aged 20-34 and the fourth most common in men in this age group.

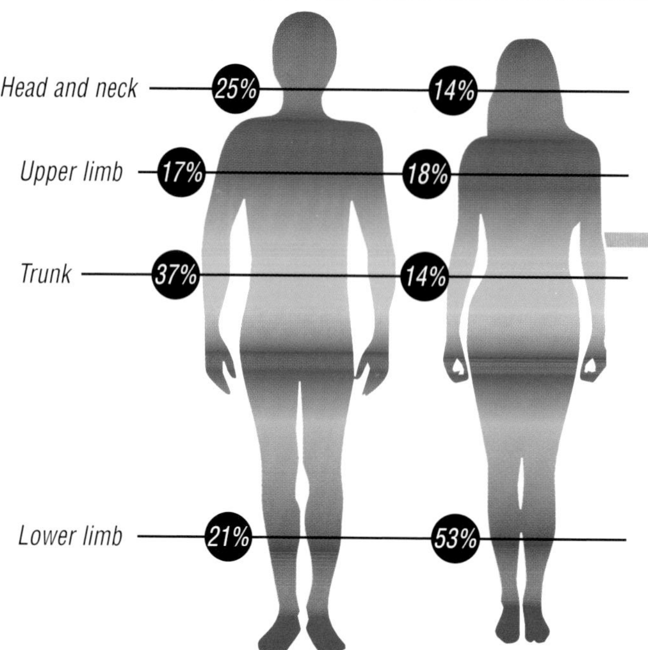

Sites of melanoma

These figures show the percentages of melanoma found on different areas of the body, for men and women. Men with melanoma tend to have it in a mole on the back or chest. For women, a mole on the lower leg is most commonly affected.

- Survival depends very much on how early the cancer is found. The stage of the cancer is calculated by measuring the thickness of the melanoma and seeing whether the cancer has spread. Survival for stage 1 (a very thin melanoma with no spread) is more than 90 per cent for five years. Survival for stage 4 (when the melanoma is much thicker or the cancer has spread) is only 20-30 per cent for five years.
- The exact cause of melanoma is not known. It is thought that exposure to sunlight – UV radiation – may damage the immune systems in the skin, allowing cells to multiply unchecked.
- People with the highest risk of melanoma are those with very fair skin, many freckles, many moles of different shapes and sizes, fair or red hair, and skin that burns easily. People with a close relative who has had a melanoma have double the risk of getting a melanoma themselves.

Watch your moles!

Major signs *to look out for are: a mole is getting darker or larger, it has developed a ragged outline, its colour is variable (i.e. darker in some parts and lighter in others).*

Minor signs: *a mole becomes inflamed or red, it starts bleeding, oozing or crusting, it starts to itch, it is bigger than your other moles.*

- Worrying moles should be removed. If the mole is found to be a melanoma, it is examined and measured under the microscope and scans are done to test whether the melanoma has spread to other parts of the body.
- Surgery is the most important treatment for melanoma. After the initial removal and testing, a further operation is needed to take away a wider area of skin. This is done to be certain that there are no remaining melanoma cells. Sometimes a skin graft is needed to repair the area. If the lymph glands near to the melanoma are large, they will also be removed. For melanomas found early, this is likely to be the only treatment needed. If the cancer has spread, chemotherapy (page 38) is used. A new form of cancer treatment is immunotherapy: the patient's own immune system is stimulated to try to make it recognize that the melanoma is there and fight it itself.

Education
The 'Slip Slop Slap' campaign in Australia was designed to educate people about protecting themselves from the sun.

Tour de force!

In 1999 27-year-old Lance Armstrong won the Tour de France, the world-famous cycling event. Three years earlier he had had aggressive treatment for an advanced cancer of the testicle. He won the race again in 2001.

The Facts

Testicular cancer

- Testicular cancer starts in the cells of the testicle. The most common type starts in the cells that make sperm.
- It can spread to nearby lymph glands and then, in the bloodstream, to the lungs, bones, etc.
- It is the commonest cancer in men aged 20-34 years.
- The exact cause is unknown, though much research is being done to investigate it.
- Testicular cancer has one of the best survival rates of all the cancers. Treatments are very successful. Overall the cure rate is more than 90 per cent. If the cancer is found at stage 1 or 2 (i.e. when it affects only the testicle, or the testicle and the nearest lymph glands), then survival is more than 95 per cent for five years. If the cancer is stage 3 at the time of diagnosis (i.e. it has spread further than the nearby lymph glands), then survival is still as high as 75 per cent for five years.
- Testicular cancer is most commonly first found as a painless lump on one or other testicle. Sometimes

Risk factors for testicular cancer

This cancer is commoner:

- *in undescended testicles (where the testicle has not descended into the scrotum at birth).*
- *if you have other family members who have had testicular cancer.*
- *in white men than in Afro-Caribbean men.*
- *in the 15-40 age group.*

Male genital tract

The testicle sits in the sac known as the scrotum.

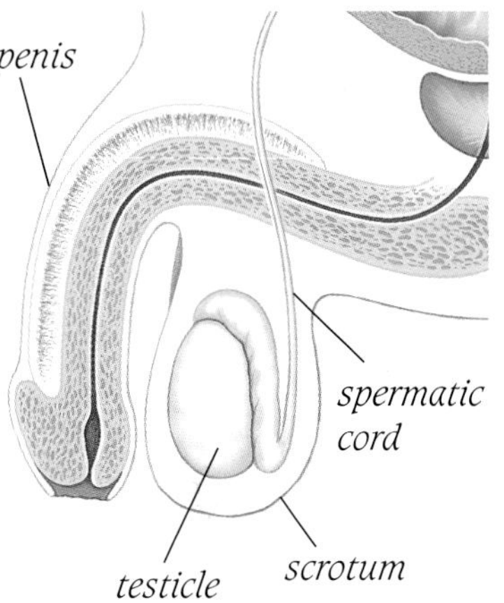

the lump is slightly uncomfortable. It may be found as a change in size of one testicle or as a noticeable difference between the two testicles. The testicle affected may feel harder than the other.

- The testicle is examined by the specialist. An ultrasound scan of the scrotum is performed, which can detect exactly where any lump is. Blood tests can show levels of different chemicals that are only present if there is a tumour.
- Treatment for this cancer is an operation to remove the whole testicle and spermatic cord, which contains the vas (the vessel that carries sperm), blood vessels and lymphatic vessels. The lymph glands in the groin may also be removed. Radiotherapy (page 36) may be given, even for the earliest stage of the disease, to kill any cancer cells in the lymph glands. Chemotherapy (page 38) is sometimes used in stage 2 disease and always used if the tumour has spread further than the lymph glands.

'I'm a keen cyclist and followed Lance Armstrong through the Tour de France. I was amazed to hear that he'd been treated for testicular cancer. I thought you died if you had cancer and there he is, winning that race! It made me think.' (Joel)

This chapter has given details of the commonest adult and young people's cancers. The same kind of details for all other types of cancer can be found by using the sources of information listed on page 62.

4 Treating cancer
Cure, control and relief

Cancer is treated in a number of ways. Most people with cancer will have more than one type of treatment.

Surgery

Sixty per cent of people with cancer will have an operation of some sort. Surgery was the first and, for many years, the only way to treat cancer. For small, solid tumours that have not spread to nearby tissue or further around the body, surgery can offer a cure.

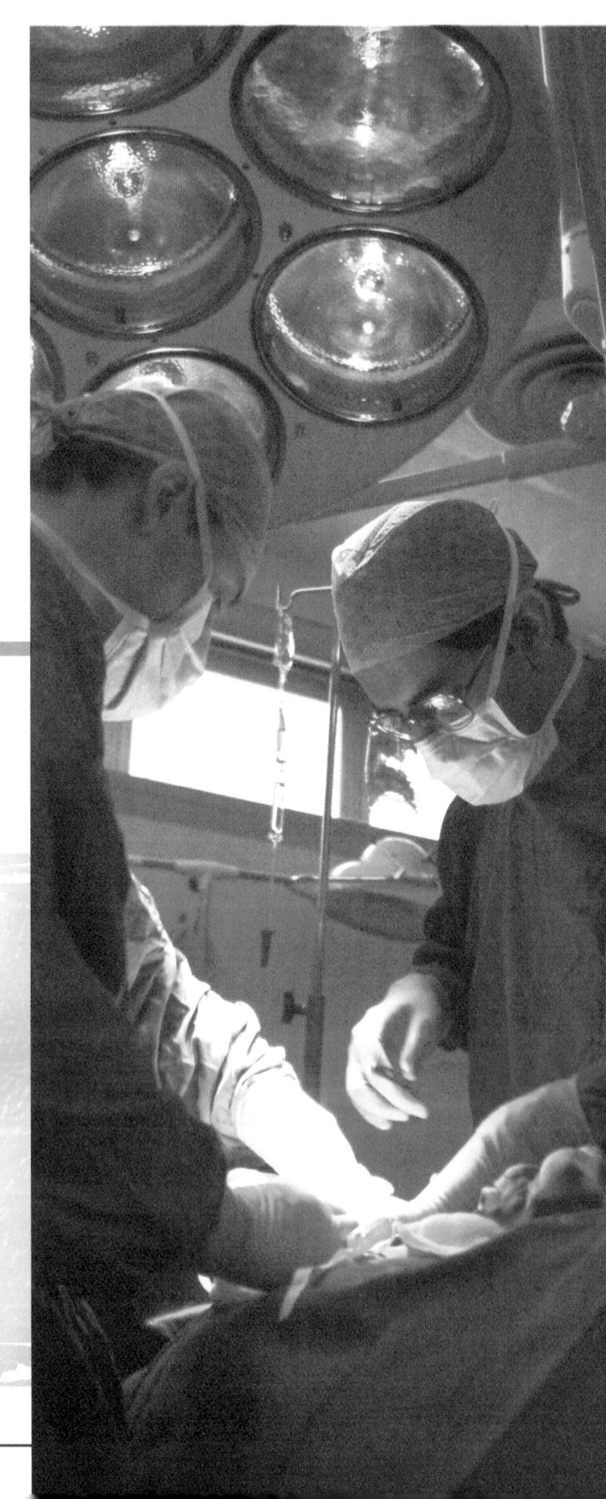

In the operating theatre
This patient is having a cancer operation whilst asleep under a general anaesthetic.

Cancer operations

As shown by the examples on page 35, operations may be used for:

- *diagnosing cancer*
- *assessing the damage (this is part of 'staging')*
- *removing a tumour*
- *relieving symptoms (this is called 'palliative surgery')*
- *repairing damage (this is called 'reconstructive surgery').*

Diagnosis

Rick had the mole on his shoulder removed under a local anaesthetic – so Rick was awake the whole time. The anaesthetic was injected into the skin near the mole, to make the area numb. The mole could then be cut out, without Rick feeling anything. The mole was then examined under a microscope to diagnose whether it was cancer or not.

Assessing damage

'I noticed glands in my neck. They have been removed and it is a lymphoma – a tumour of lymph glands. Now I'm going to have another operation to remove my spleen, to see if the cancer has spread.' (Jo)

Relieving symptoms

Frank has lung cancer. 'I have had part of my lung removed to try to improve my breathing. I know it won't cure me. It is called palliative treatment.'

Removing a tumour

'I had a lump on my testicle. The lump was found to be cancer but at a very early stage. The whole testicle has been removed and they say I should be fine. I don't need any other treatment.' (Neil)

Repairing damage

'I had a mastectomy for breast cancer. Now I have had an operation to rebuild my breast so I can feel more like a normal woman again. It is called reconstructive surgery. I have heard that nowadays women can have the reconstruction done at the same time as the mastectomy.' (Sue)

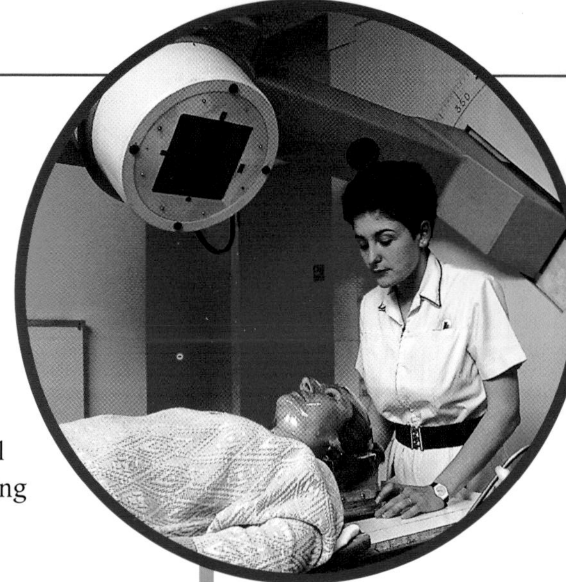

Radiotherapy

About 50-60 per cent of cancer sufferers receive radiotherapy as part of their treatment. This involves targeting the cancer cells with radiation, like X-rays. It sounds strange that radiation is used to *treat* cancer, when we know already that radiation can *cause* cancer. Radiation can kill cancer cells by damaging the cells' DNA during cell division.

Radiotherapy kills cells that are dividing rapidly. Cancer cells divide rapidly, but so do other cell types in the body, such as the cells that make blood. Radiotherapy cannot distinguish between the two and so some of the body's normal cells are also damaged by the treatment. Cells that can be quickly killed by radiotherapy are called radiosensitive cells.

Radiotherapy
The patient is positioned so that the beam of radiation will target the cancer cells. A plastic face mask is used to keep the patient immobile.

Uses of radiotherapy in cancer treatment

- *For some cancers it is the first and only treatment used.*
- *It can be used to shrink the size of a tumour before surgery.*
- *It is used as a palliative treatment, to relieve some of the symptoms of cancer. For example, in advanced cancer, where the cancer has spread to bones, radiotherapy helps relieve bone pain.*
- *It can be used as part of the first treatment for cancer, in combination with surgery and chemotherapy, to try to kill any cancer cells that may have been left after surgery. This is common after surgery for breast cancer, where the chest wall is treated.*
- *It is often used to stop cancer cells growing in parts of the body to which the cancer commonly spreads. For example, patients with lung cancer are often given radiotherapy to the brain, because lung cancer commonly spreads to the brain. The treatment tries to stop even tiny numbers of cancer cells from growing and multiplying.*

Since the days when radiotherapy was first used to treat cancer its safety has improved. In the early days, cancers used to appear in people some years after their radiation treatment. Leukaemia was the most likely cancer to occur after radiotherapy, usually about five years later. Nowadays, the cancers to be treated are targeted better and the doses of radiation given are calculated more carefully. Modern techniques allow higher doses of radiation to be more sharply focused on the cancer. Computers are used to map the site and the size of the tumour precisely. Radiation can then be aimed from several directions to give three-dimensional treatment. The surrounding tissue is more carefully protected. Chemicals are also used to make tumours more sensitive to radiation, so that lower doses have more effect.

Preparing for radiotherapy

Joanne is being prepared to have radiotherapy after surgery for breast cancer. 'I have had my first visit to the radiotherapy department. The specialist has explained the process to me. When I have my treatment I will have to stay still for about 30 minutes. They say it's like having an X-ray. I will need to have treatments every day for about three weeks. First of all, they must calculate the dose I should have. This will depend on my size and also on how much radiation the rest of my body can stand. Then they will mark my skin with purple marks that will stay on for the whole course of treatment. It is like a temporary tattoo. It means that they will always focus the radiation on the same bit of skin. I have been warned that I will feel tired; my blood count may fall so that I become anaemic. It's frightening because they have explained all the other things that may happen like feeling sick, having a dry mouth and getting diarrhoea. The skin on my chest may turn red and dry and scaly. I will have to be careful to look after it. Radiotherapy can stop you being fertile, as it kills dividing cells including sperm and eggs. They will protect my ovaries while I am being treated. My first treatment will be next week.'

Genes and cell division

Before a cell divides, it copies all its genes exactly, so that it has twice the normal amount of genetic material (3). The doubled chromosomes separate as the cell starts to divide (4).

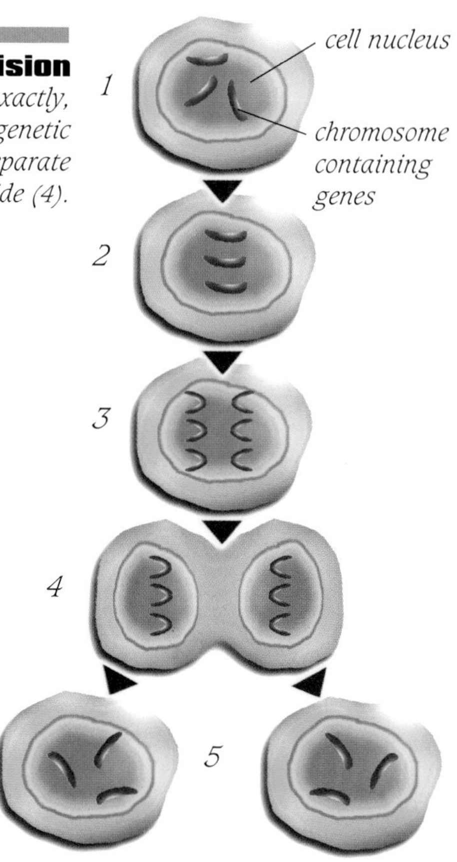

Chemotherapy

Chemotherapy is a form of cancer treatment that uses drugs to kill cancer cells. Like radiotherapy, chemotherapy attacks cells as they are dividing.

More than 90 different drugs are used in chemotherapy. Different types attack cells at different stages of the cell division cycle. Again like radiotherapy, chemotherapy cannot distinguish dividing cancer cells from dividing normal cells, but it has its greatest effect on the very rapidly dividing cancer cells.

Chemotherapy can be used in cancer treatment in the following different ways:

- to achieve a cure. The drugs may be used alone, for example in the treatment of leukaemia, or in conjunction with other treatments. For example, drugs can be given after surgery or after radiotherapy to kill any tiny number of cancer cells that may have started to spread around the body but are not yet detectable. This is known as adjuvant therapy. Also, drugs can be used to shrink the size of a tumour before surgery – this is known as neo-adjuvant therapy.

Mustard gas

The fact that chemicals can kill cells during cell division was discovered when mustard gas was used in the Second World War. People exposed to this gas were found to have fewer white blood cells in their blood. The production of white blood cells had been slowed down by the chemical attacking them during cell division.

- to control the growth and spread of cancer. Under these circumstances drugs are used to prolong a good quality of life for as long as possible.
- as a palliative therapy, to control some of the symptoms of advanced cancer when neither cure nor control is possible.

Single drugs or combinations of drugs working in slightly different ways can be used. A course of chemotherapy treatment usually takes some months. The course consists of several sessions during which the drugs are given. A session may last from a few hours to a few days. After each session there is a short rest period, often lasting a couple of weeks. The rest periods are to allow the body's normal cells to recover.

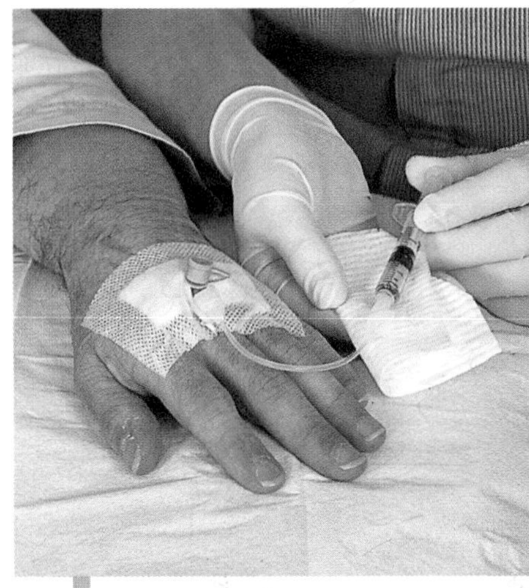

Intravenous drugs
Drugs are given into the blood via a vein in the back of the hand.

The commonest method of giving the drugs is intravenously. A tiny plastic tube is put into a vein and then the drugs are given through this tube by an intravenous (IV) drip. The drugs can then spread via the bloodstream to all parts of the body, killing cancer cells wherever they are. Many patients need many sessions of chemotherapy, and having an IV line inserted every time could be very uncomfortable. For these patients, a central line is used. This is a longer plastic tube put into one of the large veins in the chest. It is securely stitched in place and can stay in for the whole course of chemotherapy.

Lumbar puncture
Before a lumbar puncture, the patient's skin is sterilized with iodine.

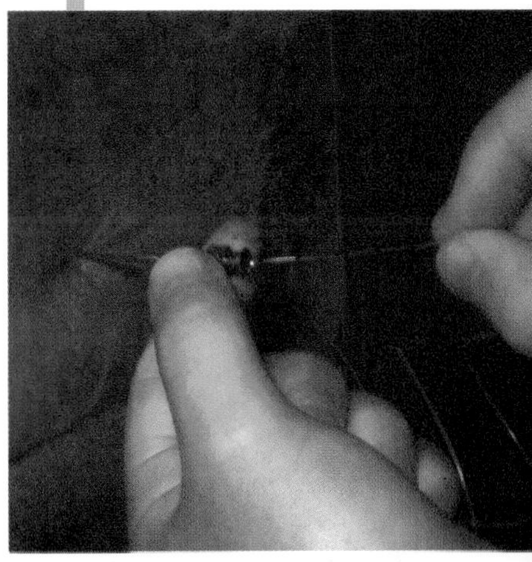

In treatments of some cancers, the chemotherapy drugs are given straight to specific parts of the body. For example, in treatment of some bladder cancers, drugs can be given through a catheter (tube) directly into the bladder. Leukaemia cells can pass into the brain, but chemotherapy drugs are often unable to get into the brain from the bloodstream. To get around this problem, the drugs can be injected directly into the cerebrospinal fluid – the fluid surrounding the brain and spinal cord – via a lumbar puncture.

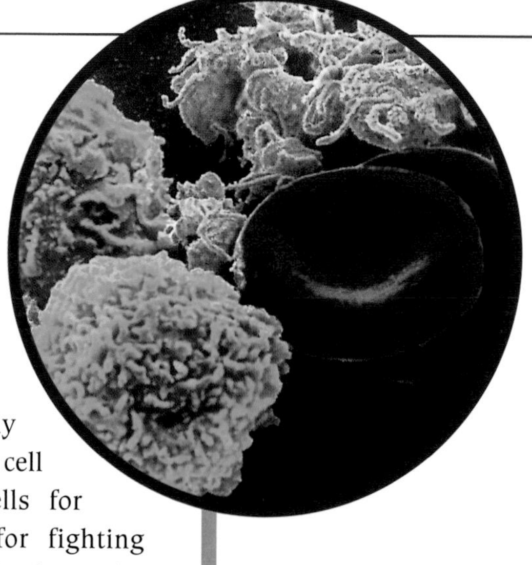

The down side

Because chemotherapy attacks the body's normal dividing cells as well as the dividing cancer cells, the treatment can have many, often unpleasant side effects.

- It can attack the blood-producing cells in the bone marrow, which are rapidly dividing. Bone marrow produces all the cell components of blood – red blood cells for carrying oxygen, white blood cells for fighting infection, and platelets for helping blood to clot. Therefore, damage to the bone marrow during chemotherapy can make a patient anaemic. It can make them prone to catching infections, and even simple infections can be dangerous because the body's own defence mechanisms are not working properly. Falling platelet numbers can make patients prone to bleeding and bruising.

Blood cell types

In this coloured electron micrograph, red blood cells are red, white blood cells are blue, and platelets are pink.

In charge of chemotherapy

'I am in charge of the chemotherapy day ward, where patients come during the day for their treatments. We try to make it as homely as possible for them. Most patients can go home at night between their treatments. The nurses and doctors have to be very careful when handling chemotherapy drugs. They are dangerous. They are designed to kill cells by damaging DNA. This is called cytotoxic. We have to take special precautions when we handle them to avoid direct contact. We could run the risk of our own cells being damaged.' (Sister Jones)

- Cells in hair follicles divide rapidly and are often attacked by chemotherapy. This means that the patient loses their hair. The hair on the head is affected more rapidly than eyebrows, pubic hair and eyelashes. Patients are often provided with a wig during their treatment.
- Cells in the gut are also dividing rapidly and can be damaged by chemotherapy. Patients may complain of a sore mouth or changes in taste. They may suffer from indigestion or feel sick and suffer vomiting. They may also get diarrhoea. All this adds to the discomfort of chemotherapy.
- Sperm in the testes and eggs in the ovaries are also rapidly dividing cells and can be damaged. Therefore, fertility can be temporarily or permanently harmed by chemotherapy. Sometimes it is possible for men to store sperm before their treatment. It can then be frozen until the man wants to have children.

Hormone therapy

Some cancers, including prostate cancer in men and breast cancer in women, need the body's hormones to keep multiplying. Women with breast cancer are often given a drug called tamoxifen which blocks the effect of the female hormone oestrogen.

Hopes for the future

Many research groups around the world are trying to improve and find new methods for treating cancer. Patients who are prepared to try therapies that have not been fully tested are entered into 'clinical trials'. This is the way by which scientists work out whether treatments will be effective, using real patients as guinea pigs.

Discoveries bring hope for sufferers

Gene therapy no longer just science fiction

Scientists have tried to introduce rogue genes into cancer cells by infecting them with a virus carrying the rogue gene. This gene then makes the cell self-destruct.

Laser light fires lethal weapon for cancer

Experiments are being done to make cancer cells sensitive to light by treating them with a chemical agent. The cells can then be destroyed by a focused laser light beam.

Effective cancer vaccine found

THE PRINCIPLE of immunotherapy is to try to boost the patient's immune system to recognize the cancer cells in his body as abnormal and fight them.

Jake's hopes for a stem cell transplant

Jake has had a lymphoma – a cancer of the lymph glands. It has not responded to ordinary chemotherapy. He has one last chance for a cure. He will have to have such powerful chemotherapy to eliminate the cancer that his bone marrow will be wiped out. He would not survive without a bone marrow, so he will need a transplant. He can either be given a bone marrow transplant from a donor, or he will have what is called a stem cell transplant. Stem cells are blood cells at the earliest stage of development. They have the capability to become any of the three types of blood cell.

The first step will be for Jake to be given a drug that partially switches off his bone marrow. Then, during the bone marrow's recovery phase, a cell growth factor will be given to dramatically increase the number of stem cells produced. These will then appear in the blood and can be collected simply by removing some of Jake's blood. After that, powerful chemotherapy will be given to wipe out all Jake's bone marrow. The stem cells will then be given as replacements through a drip.

Jake says: 'I'm hoping to have a stem cell transplant. If I need a donor bone marrow transplant, I know it takes several weeks for the new bone marrow cells to settle into my body and start working normally. During that time I would have to spend all my time alone in a hospital room. My family could visit, but not if they are unwell. The nurses have to be very careful not to bring any infection into the room. You see, until the new bone marrow works properly, I could catch any old infection and it could kill me because I would not be able to fight it. It all sounds boring, lonely and very frightening. But if I have to, I will manage.'

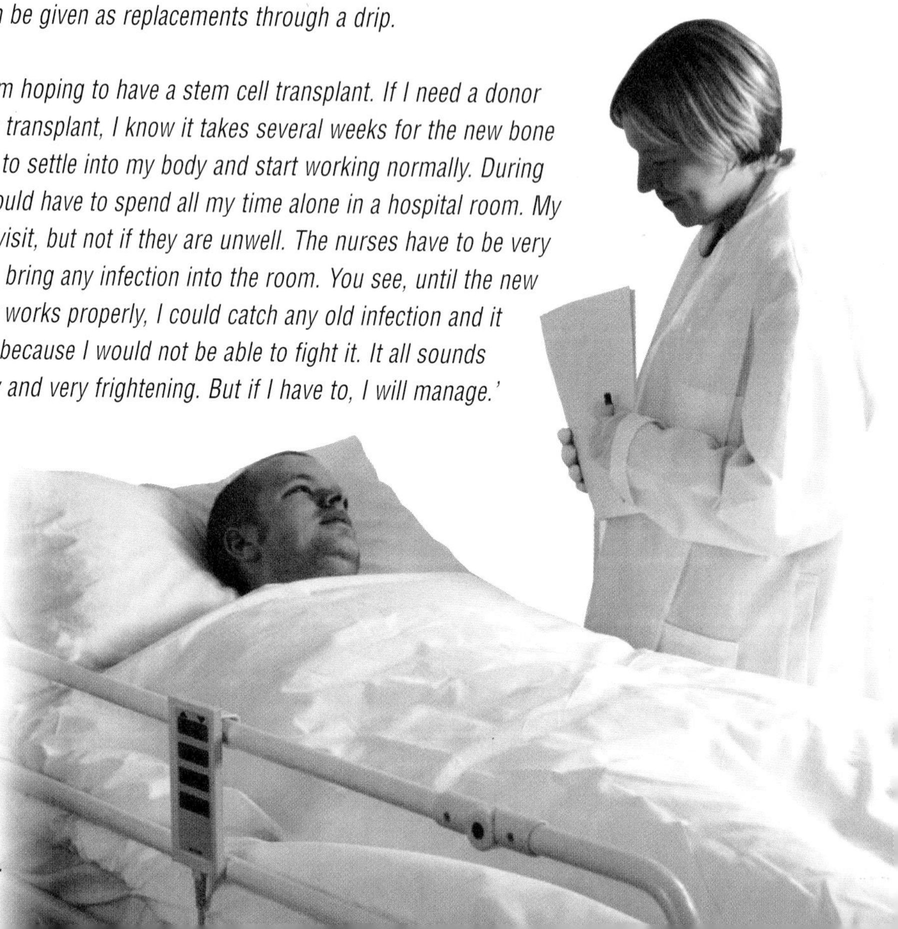

Alternative and complementary therapies

Patients for whom standard cancer treatment is failing often seek help elsewhere. An 'alternative therapy' is an unproven treatment used in place of standard treatment. Many claims are made for such treatments. Patients should beware claims that a treatment cures all cancers, that conventional treatment is a waste of time and that the treatment follows a secret recipe known only to a chosen few. These claims are likely to be very unrealistic.

A 'complementary therapy' is a treatment used in addition to standard treatment, to help the patient feel good about themselves and tolerate the rigours of surgery, radiotherapy and chemotherapy. Complementary therapies are often excellent at reducing pain and fear and improving quality of life. They include aromatherapy, massage, art and music therapy, yoga and meditation.

Complementary therapies

Massage and art therapy are two examples of complementary therapies that help improve a patient's sense of wellbeing.

5 Cancer prevention
Choosing the best lifestyle

Estimates vary, but possibly up to 80 per cent of cancers could be prevented by modifying our lifestyle and environment. At present, in the developed world, one in three people will develop cancer at some stage in their life. Focusing on prevention could mean fewer cancer deaths and fewer new cases of cancer. Preventing cancer is called primary prevention. Finding cancer early so that it can be cured is called secondary prevention. So what can you do to help yourself?

The bad diet
Fried egg, chips, burgers and alcohol are low-fibre and high-fat foods. A diet with excessive amounts of these foods may increase your cancer risk.

Don't smoke

Do not start smoking. If you are a smoker, think of quitting. If you are a non-smoker, do not spend a lot of time in the presence of smokers, as passive smoking also increases cancer risk. There are 30-40 carcinogenic chemicals in smoked tobacco. Smoking is a direct cause of lung cancer and amongst the causes of many other cancers (see page 16). Most people who develop lung cancer will die from the disease. This cancer has one of the poorest records for successful treatment. Large numbers of people stopping smoking would have a significant effect on the numbers developing and dying from cancer.

Don't drink to excess

The recommended safe limits for alcohol intake are 2-3 units of alcohol per day for men and 1-2 units per day for women. The mechanism by which alcohol causes cancer is not fully understood. Cancers in the mouth, throat, voice box, oesophagus and liver are all much commoner in people who drink to excess. It may be that, when alcohol is broken down or metabolized in the body, one of the

How smoking and drinking increase your risk of cancer of the oesophagus

0 alcohol	2 glasses wine per day	>4 glasses wine per day
0 cigarettes	20 cigarettes per day	>20 cigarettes per day
=	=	=
Very low risk	5 x average risk	40 x average risk

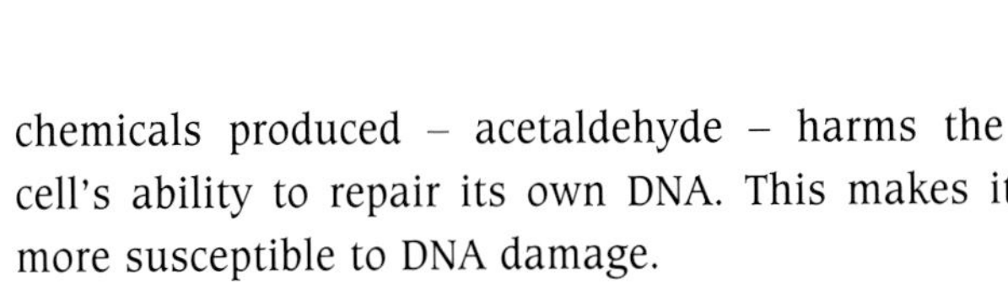

chemicals produced – acetaldehyde – harms the cell's ability to repair its own DNA. This makes it more susceptible to DNA damage.

If you smoke *and* drink, the situation is worse. This is particularly true for cancer of the oesophagus, as the table above shows. It is thought that alcohol acts as a co-carcinogen: the effect of alcohol on the cells of the oesophagus makes them more sensitive to the carcinogenic chemicals in tobacco.

The good diet
A low-fat diet with plenty of fresh vegetables is thought to help keep your cancer risk low.

Watch your diet and your weight

It is becoming increasingly clear that some factors in our diet may keep cells healthy and protect us against cancer. Other factors may be directly harmful to cells. A huge investigation of this subject is being conducted in Europe. The European Prospective Investigation of Cancer (EPIC) study is looking at 400,000 people in nine countries. Their diets are being examined and they are being monitored to look at the cancers they develop and whether there are links between the type of cancer and particular aspects of diet. So far, there is evidence for the influence of diet in bowel and breast cancer, but diet is also thought to contribute to the risk of cancers of the lung, prostate, stomach, oesophagus and pancreas.

The Good

Diet and bowel cancer

People who eat fruit and vegetables regularly and have a high-fibre diet have more regular bowel actions, a heavier weight of faeces and less constipation. All these factors reduce the risk of bowel cancer. People who eat a lot of red meat (pork, beef and lamb) and processed meat (sausages, hamburgers, and smoked, cured and salted meats) are more likely to develop bowel cancer. It is possible that chemicals formed when red meat and animal fat are cooked may be partly responsible for cell changes in the gut.

The Bad

The dietary message is:

- Eat at least five portions of fruit and vegetables every day.
- Have a high-fibre diet. Fibre is found in unprocessed cereals, bran and root vegetables.
- Have only small amounts of refined sugar.
- Cut back on animal fat in dairy products and red meat.
- Reduce salt in your diet. Use herbs and spices instead.
- Use small amounts of vegetable oils for cooking.
- Avoid mouldy or charred food.
- Avoid being overweight. Keep your body mass index (weight divided by height squared) between 18 and 25.

Stomach cancer

Chemicals called oxidative-free radicals, found in the stomach after eating, are known to damage DNA. Vegetables and fruit are sources of antioxidants, particularly carotene and vitamin E, which can protect against this DNA damage. People who eat 5-20 portions of fruit and vegetables per week have half the risk of cancer of the stomach compared with those who do not.

Keep physically active

The benefits of physical activity have been researched most in relation to bowel cancer. Active women were found to have half the bowel cancer risk of inactive women. Activity reduces the time taken for faeces to pass through the colon. This means that the colon is exposed for less long to possible carcinogens in faeces. Activity also has a good effect on digestive agents such as insulin, prostaglandin and bile acids. These are all known to influence growth and proliferation of cells in the colon.

A woman's production of sex hormone influences her risk of breast cancer and cancer of the endometrium (the lining of the uterus). Physical activity may alter the production, breakdown and excretion of sex hormones. It also helps to keep body weight normal. Being active and of normal weight could reduce breast cancer risk by 30 per cent.

Making oestrogen

Most breast cancers need the hormone oestrogen for the cancer to thrive. Another cancer that needs oestrogen is cancer of the lining of the uterus – the endometrium. Oestrogen is produced normally in the ovaries. But observations and scientific investigations have shown that extra oestrogen is also produced in fatty tissue. Women who have passed the menopause and who are very overweight have approximately double the normal risk of breast cancer. Obese women also have a higher incidence of endometrial cancer.

The health freak

- Walks to and from school.
- Goes to trampoline club.
- Does football training once a week and plays a football match once a week.
- Swims and plays tennis as leisure activities.

The couch potato

- Gets a lift to school every day.
- Watches TV most nights.
- Goes to watch a football match on Saturdays.
- Listens to music and plays Play Station for leisure activities.

Take exercise every day and do at least one hour of vigorous exercise per week.

Beware of the sun

Skin cancers are linked with the amount of ultraviolet radiation from the sun that reaches the skin. Most can be prevented by following the skin protection rules. You are more likely to develop skin cancer if you have had frequent episodes of sunburn but also if you have been exposed to the sun for long periods during work and play. You are at higher risk if you have very fair, freckly skin, light-coloured eyes, fair or red hair and skin that burns easily. You are least at risk if you have pigmented skin.

The skin protection rules

- *Avoid the midday sun – between 11 am and 3 pm.*
- *Seek natural shade. Sit under a tree or under shelter.*
- *Wear cover-up clothing such as T-shirts, hats and sunglasses.*
- *Use a broad-spectrum sunscreen – SPF 15 or higher, with protection against UVB but also with additional UVA protection.*
- *Reapply sunscreens frequently – say, every two hours.*
- *Remember that sunscreen can be wiped off (e.g. when drying with a towel), washed off (e.g. when swimming) or sweated off.*

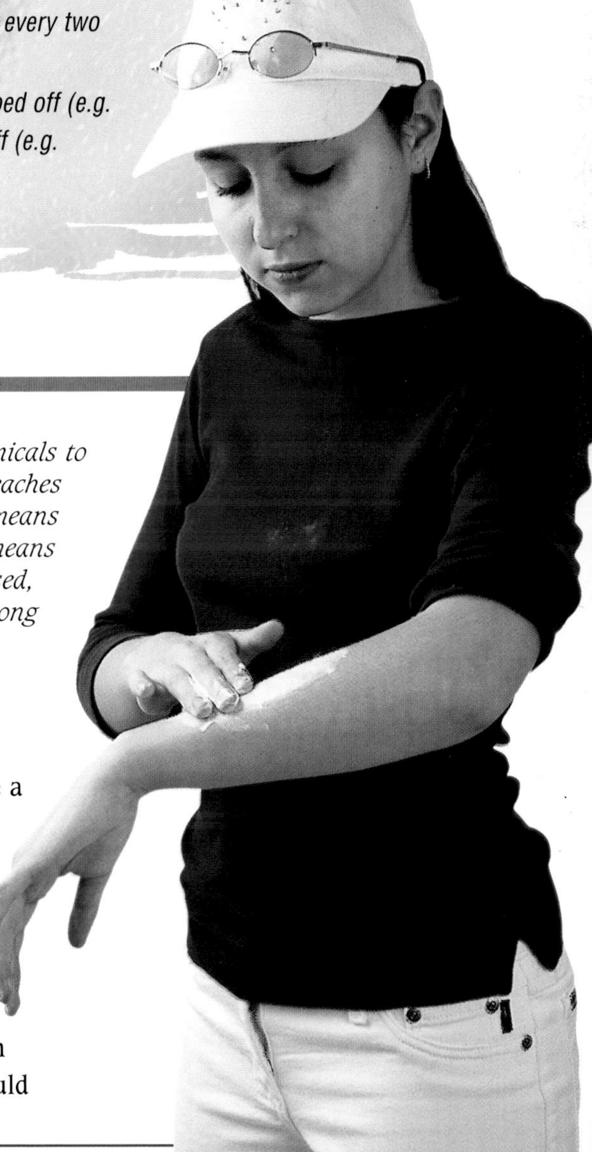

Cover up!

Sunscreens work by using chemicals to absorb UV radiation before it reaches the skin. 'SPF' on sunscreens means sun protection factor. SPF 15 means that, when this sunscreen is used, the skin will take 15 times as long to burn as without sunscreen.

Avoid infections that can cause cancer

Do not be sexually promiscuous. If you have a sexual relationship, always practise 'safe sex'. Most cancers of the cervix in women are caused by some types of the human papilloma or wart virus. Infection with this virus is more common in women who have many sexual partners. The risk of catching a sexually transmitted infection can be reduced by practising safe sex. You should only have full penetrative sexual intercourse when you know you are ready and you feel confident that you are in a stable relationship. Always use a condom when you have sex, regardless of any other forms of contraception that you use. This is the only way of protecting against infection during intercourse.

Hepatitis B infection increases the risk of liver cancer. If you live in a part of the world where hepatitis B is common, or if you are travelling to such a place, make sure you are protected by having a hepatitis B immunization. Hepatitis B can be transmitted sexually and by infected blood. Again, the message is to practise safe sex, and also to avoid handling dirty needles.

Be careful of dangerous substances

Chemicals used in the workplace may have the potential to be carcinogenic. Make sure that you follow any safety instructions carefully, such as wearing protective clothing. Do not cut corners and take risks.

'It was embarrassing at school when we were told how to check our testicles. Now I'm glad because I do it every now and again and it makes me feel more secure.'
(Richard, age 17)

Be aware of your body

Early detection of cancer makes cure far more likely. Doctors know that, for certain cancers such as breast

Men: be testicle-aware

- *Both testicles should be roughly the same weight. Hold them in your hands to check. It is normal for one testicle to look smaller than the other and to sit higher in the scrotum than the other.*
- *Look for lumps on the front or side of the testicle. Roll the testicle between your thumb and finger. It should be smooth. The soft, tender tube at the back is normal. It is a mass of sperm-carrying vessels called the epididymis.*
- *Check that one testicle has not become more swollen or firm than the other and that there is no unusual difference between the two.*
- *Notice any pain or discomfort.*

cancer, bowel cancer, testicular cancer, skin cancer and cancer of the cervix, early detection of tumours saves lives. So you should be aware of your body and report any changes to your doctor. Be generally aware of early signs of cancer:

'My Mum taught me how to keep an eye on my breasts. I do a check every two or three months just after my period. It makes me feel secure.' (Sarah, age 23)

- Watch out for any new lumps.
- Keep an eye on moles in case they change.
- Watch out for any abnormal bleeding.
- Respond if you have a persistent problem such as weight loss, a cough that won't go away, a hoarse voice that doesn't get better, altered bowels.
- Women should check their breasts, looking out for the symptoms explained on page 23. Men should check their testicles.

Respond to invitations to be screened for cancer

Cancer screening means using medical tests on healthy people to detect cancers at an early stage, before there are any noticeable symptoms. There are reliable tests for early detection of breast cancer and cervical cancer, and screening is widely available for these.

Cervical smear
In most countries, all women between the ages of about 20 and 65 are offered a cervical smear (pap test) every three to five years.

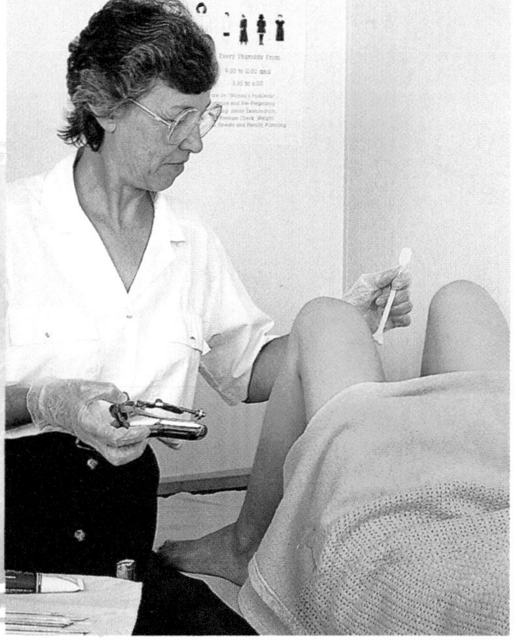

Smear tests

Routine screening by smear test was first investigated in Iceland in 1965. By 1970, 80 per cent of women aged 25-70 had had one smear test. Over the next 20 years death rates from cervical cancer fell by 60 per cent. The smear test can find cell changes that are pre-cancerous – that is, they have not yet become cancer. These can then be treated effectively to prevent cancer from developing.

Cancer markers

Much research is being carried out into ways of detecting cancers early. Some cancers make their own markers – 'biomarkers' – which can then be detected by blood tests. For example, it is possible to measure a biomarker for prostate cancer, called the prostate specific antigen or PSA. There is also a chemical biomarker for ovarian cancer, called Ca 125.

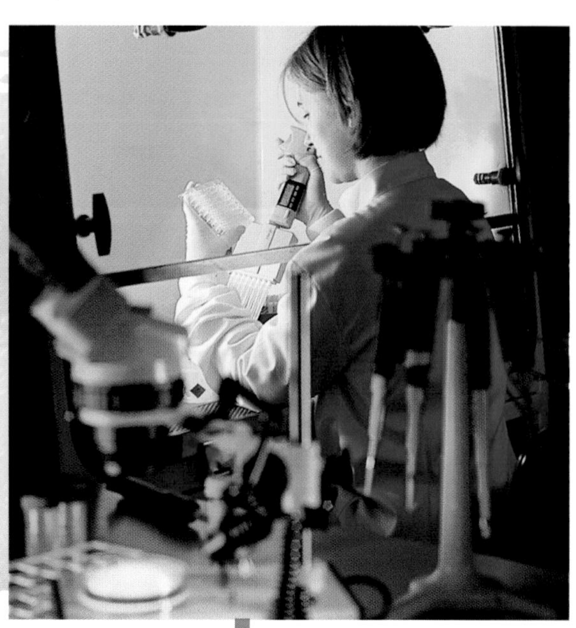

Cancer research

A researcher works with cancer cells in a biological safety cabinet. The cells are being grown to see how they respond to anti-cancer drugs.

In the UK, there is a national screening programme for breast cancer. All women aged 50-65 years are offered a mammogram (breast X-ray) every three years to see if there is a small tumour present that has not yet been felt.

Various techniques are being investigated for screening people for colon or bowel cancer. People at high risk, because they have a family history of this cancer, are recommended to have regular colonoscopies (page 26). Attempts are being made to screen whole populations. One method is to examine stool samples for small traces of blood. This blood may have come from a bowel tumour. If blood is present, then the person needs further tests such as a colonoscopy or sigmoidoscopy to look at the inside of the colon.

Ovarian cancer is a relatively common female cancer with a very poor outlook, as it is usually only found when it is very advanced. Detecting it earlier would allow many more women with ovarian cancer to survive. Techniques include examination by a doctor, ultrasound scan of the pelvis to look at the ovaries, and measurement of a biomarker called Ca 125. No technique has yet been found to be ideal.

6 Living with cancer
How families cope

Jane is 45. Through her story, we can see many of the issues that confront people with cancer and their families.

'When Mum told us all that she had cancer, I just put my arm round her. I don't know if that was right, but it saved having to say anything. All the time she was in hospital I felt numb. I didn't tell anyone. It seemed disloyal and anyway what could they do?'
(Jessica, age 16)

A year with cancer

'About a year ago I was told that I had breast cancer. I needed a mastectomy. I couldn't believe it. My husband David was great, but I found I couldn't talk to him. Thoughts came rushing into my head. What about the children? Who will look after them if I die? I cannot bear the thought of cancer treatment. It's not worth it. I won't be me any more. Luckily, the hospital had a nurse counsellor who went through all these issues with David and me. She let me talk, and cry. Then she helped me think about how I would deal with it.

We decided that we had to tell the kids straight away. Jessica is 16, Richard 13 and Paul is 10. Jessica was marvellous and put her arm round me. Richard didn't know how to react. I could tell he was angry that we would miss our holiday. Paul ran off to his room. David had a long session with him later. He had worried that it was all his fault, because I'm always shouting at him about his untidy room. He knew about people dying from cancer and thought I would be dead next week. But he also didn't trust that he wouldn't die himself.

After the operation I hated myself. I couldn't touch myself or look at myself in the mirror. I thought this new person would never be me again. I couldn't imagine ever letting David cuddle me. Anyway, I was sure he would reject me when he saw my scar.

Next I had to have radiotherapy – going to the hospital every day for 3-4 weeks. I was really tired and there were times when I couldn't bear the kids scrapping. I wanted peace – but I wanted to be with them too. We had to be careful that their lives stayed as normal as possible. It was really difficult talking to friends about having cancer, because I didn't know how they would react. Having them help me out in practical ways, like transporting the children or cooking meals, seemed to make it easier for us all.

It still wasn't over. A cancer specialist called an oncologist talked me through all the treatment options. My cancer was quite advanced, so I needed more than the operation and radiotherapy to try to improve my chances of surviving long term. But he couldn't give me guarantees – just percentage chances. The uncertainty is hard to deal with. If I have a 60 per cent chance of survival, will I be one of the lucky ones? The nurse counsellor advised about getting information and talking to people to try to sort out things in my own mind.

It seemed best to really fight the cancer for everyone's sake, so I went for chemotherapy too. There seemed to be no break from problems. Our lives had been completely taken over by my cancer. Jessica was great most of the time and helped as much as she could, but she resented not having a normal home life. She wanted to get out with her friends but instead kept having to mind her brothers for me. I had to be careful not to expect too much. I was worried about Richard because he wouldn't talk. He got into some trouble at school, which was unlike him. Paul's school was really good at helping him to deal with his fears.

'Sometimes it was hard to talk to my brothers but at other times we were all together. We would all laugh hysterically at something together if we were home alone. There were also days when I felt "Why should I have to do all this stuff at home?" Then I would feel really guilty.' (Jessica)

Chemotherapy was horrible. I lost all my hair. I took Jessica with me to choose a wig and we had a laugh, but wearing it is a different matter. It's hot and itchy and just not my hair. For a week after each session of chemo, I felt sick and so tired that I could hardly move. That made it very difficult to keep everything going – David's job, school, homework, activities.

Some people I wouldn't have expected have turned out to be the best listeners or the most able to judge when to tell a joke, when to shut up and when to help out practically. I know it's hard for everyone else too, but some people drive me mad. They shower me with gifts but never come near me.

'I never felt I was doing or saying the right thing at home. The counsellor at school gave me tips about how to help Mum and listen to her, and said it was OK just to be with her and not talk all the time. She said none of it was my fault and I was allowed to have my own life too.' (Jessica)

When I was in the middle of chemo, I realized that Jessica was never bringing her friends home. We had a chat and I learned that her friends were talking about me and upsetting her. So I got them all round for pizza when I was feeling reasonable and we talked all about cancer. I showed them my head without hair and talked about my treatment.

David and I have had some bad moments. I got very sad when he kept shouting at the kids. I knew he was trying to protect me, but it upset me more to see them unhappy. He was also stressed but tried not to show it in case it upset me. One evening we had a shouting session and both ended up in tears, but it cleared the air. Since then we have been able to share our feelings much better. I couldn't have gone through it all without him and the kids. David came with me to all my appointments. He made sure I asked all my questions. He helped me to express my fears and to tell the doctors and nurses if I felt awful. I always felt guilty about complaining.

For nearly a year, all our lives were turned upside-down by cancer. Now I'm beginning to see that some of the hurt and trauma has had a good side. We have grown together as a family. We have all learnt to express ourselves and be at one with our emotions. I have re-evaluated life. I think my priorities are different now. I can see beauty in little things and get real joy from just a good laugh with the kids. Material things like the car and big holidays just seem unimportant. Maybe there is a silver lining to cancer.'

Children with cancer

There are particular issues and dilemmas when a child has cancer. Living day to day with cancer, the treatment regimes and trips to hospital can be stressful for families.

- The child with cancer will feel frightened and uncertain. He or she will want answers to many questions, but may not know how or whom to ask.
- To children, hospitals may simply mean pain. A child may be fearful of pain. Hospital staff and play therapists are skilled at helping children talk about what they are feeling. Sometimes drawing pictures helps to describe things.
- Family life is disrupted. The parents and the sick child will spend a lot of time at hospital, maybe a long way from home. The other children in the family may feel ignored.
- It can be difficult to involve grandparents and they may be very distressed but feel unable to contribute.
- The situation can put great pressure on the relationship between the child's parents.
- Some cancer treatment leaves the patient vulnerable to serious infection. For this reason, a child may need to be kept isolated, even though he or she feels fit enough to continue normal activities.
- Schooling needs to continue while the child is having treatment. Many hospitals have school in hospital. The child's own school will be able to provide work to do at home.
- It can be hard for parents of a sick child to maintain discipline. But doing so gives structure to life, which is usually comforting to someone in distress.

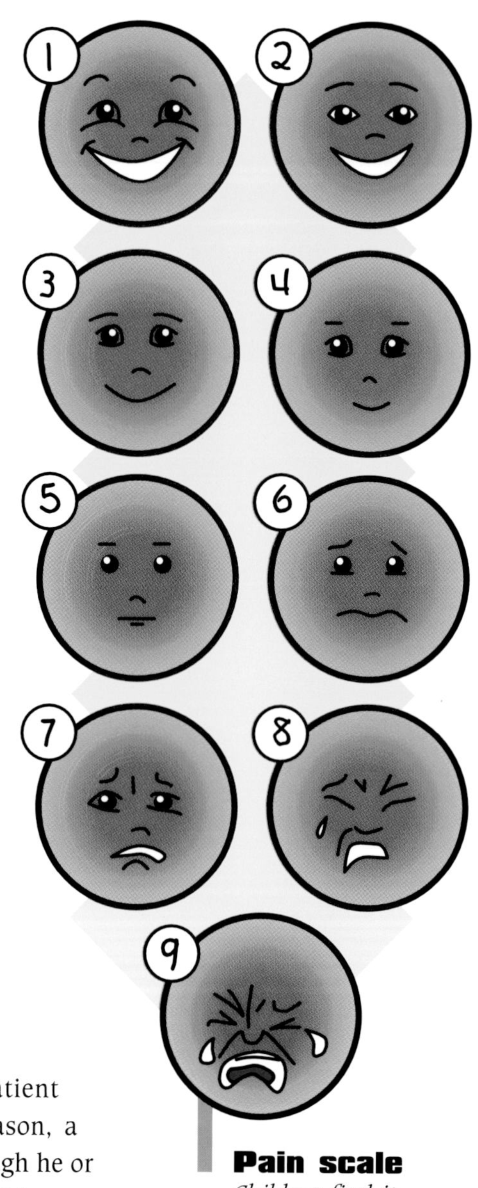

Pain scale
Children find it difficult to describe pain. Hospitals may use a set of pictures like these. A child can point at the face that expresses how he or she is feeling.

Dying from cancer

Chris's father Jim died a month ago from an advanced melanoma.

'Dad had a nasty mole on his back a couple of years ago and the doctors found that the cancer had already spread. He had loads of treatment and was rarely able to get to work. Then this year he started feeling sicker. The cancer had spread to his liver and bones and lungs. Gradually he was unable to move around the house much and then he took to his bed. He had become just skin and bones, apart from his big belly that had filled with fluid. This made it really difficult for him to be comfortable in bed and didn't help his breathing. He lost his appetite and at the end was only able to sip drinks.

We had a family discussion. Dad knew he was dying and wanted to stay at home with us. We all decided we could manage. We had help from doctors who sorted out the medicines to make life as comfortable as possible for Dad. Nurses came to make sure we were coping and told us about turning Dad to keep his skin good and avoid pressure sores and about looking after his mouth to keep it moist. We also had special nurses who sat with him some nights so that we could get some sleep. Social services brought all sorts of things to make life easier, like a walking frame when he was still able to get up.

Sharing memories

At the beginning of Dad's illness, we spent time talking about things we remembered doing together.

Dad's pain seemed to be well controlled. He was given morphine first as tablets. Then, as swallowing became harder, they brought a syringe pump to give him a mixture of morphine and other drugs to stop sickness and keep him calm and dry up the bubbly mucus in his mouth. The drugs are mixed in a syringe which is attached to a needle and delivers the drugs slowly over 24 hours, just under the skin.

Before Dad got so sick that he couldn't talk and was barely conscious, we all managed to talk together about his funeral. It seemed strange, but it probably helped us to take in that he was going to die. We had shared a lot together over the two years. We took family photos. Dad wrote each of us a story to remember him by. We had some good laughs. It wasn't all gloomy.

I had expected the last days to be the worst, but it was very peaceful. Over two days Dad slipped more and more into unconsciousness. He still seemed aware of us. His eyelids would move or we could feel pressure from his hand. We took turns to sit with him, sponge him down, moisten his lips. Nobody talked much. Other people like neighbours seemed to appear and made sure that we ate and drank. He died at 6 o'clock on the Thursday evening. His breathing had become very shallow and infrequent, then he just didn't take another breath. We all gave him a little kiss on the forehead to say goodbye. We still sat with him for a bit. It seemed hard to leave him.

Flowers
We chose flowers for the funeral that we knew Dad would like.

Eventually someone called the doctor who confirmed that Dad had died. Then the undertaker came and, when we were all ready, Dad was moved to the undertakers' building. I think Dad's body was kept in a fridge there until the funeral.

We all did our little bit at the funeral. I read Dad's favourite poem. My sister played her violin. Mum did a reading and Dad's brother talked about all the great things Dad had done in his life.

We all seemed to react to his death in a slightly different way. At first I felt numb. I don't suppose it had sunk in. Then I felt angry that cancer had hit my dad. Why me? It wasn't fair. Now I think I am just in the very sad stage. They say that the pain gets easier with time. I'm not sure I believe that yet.'

Carers

There are many sources of help for cancer patients and their families. In the UK, the GP takes overall responsibility, prescribing drugs and arranging home services or admission to a hospice or hospital, according to the patient's wishes. Community nurses give nursing support at home, change dressings, administer drugs, and advise on skin and mouth care. Specialist nurses, such as Macmillan nurses, have special expertise in managing pain and other symptoms and also give emotional support to patients and their families. Marie Curie nurses offer night care, to give relatives a break. Occupational therapists and physiotherapists provide aids such as wheelchairs and commodes and help with mobility, exercises and pain-relieving massage. Social care includes home helps, for cleaning, cooking and shopping, and care attendants who help with washing and dressing and sit with patients to give relatives a break.

Hospices

A hospice is an organization that specializes in the care of people living with cancer or dying from cancer. Their skill is in control of pain and other symptoms and also in offering support to patients and their families. A hospice may have home care teams, or patients may go to the hospice for the day, for a change of scene and a chance to meet others. Many hospices also offer periods of residential care.

Bereavement

When someone close to us dies, we enter a period of grieving. There are many components to grief. Everyone reacts differently, but most people experience all the usual feelings at different times and for different periods. Sometimes a person's grief does not resolve and they will need help, maybe with anti-depressant treatment, to enable them to move on.

There are many organizations that help people deal with bereavement. Details of these are available through the cancer charities listed on page 62.

Stages of grieving

The usual process of grieving follows a pattern:

- *Numbness*
- *Denial*
- *Anger and guilt*
- *Pining and yearning*
- *Depression*
- *Gradual recovery*

Glossary

anaemia paleness and tiredness caused by a lack of red blood cells.

antibiotics drugs or medicines that kill bacteria. They do not kill viruses.

biopsy taking a sample of tissue so that the cells can be examined in detail under a microscope.

blood cells White blood cells fight infection. Red blood cells carry oxygen in the blood. Platelets help blood to clot.

bowel the large intestine; that is, the section of intestine stretching from the appendix to the anus, in which faeces are formed by the body reabsorbing water. An alternative name for the bowel is the colon.

bronchoscopy investigation of the windpipe performed by passing a telescopic tube through the mouth into the airway. Biopsies from the lung can be taken through the tube.

cancer screening a method of testing large groups of people to see if they have a particular cancer; e.g. using mammograms for women aged 50-65 years, to test for breast cancer.

carcinogen something that produces a cancerous change in a cell, such as a chemical, radiation or infections.

cervix neck of the womb or uterus.

chemotherapy cancer treatment using drugs to kill the rapidly dividing cancer cells.

chromosome The nucleus of each human cell contains 23 pairs of chromosomes. This is the cell's genetic material. *See also* gene.

colon *See* bowel.

colonoscopy This is very similar to sigmoidoscopy, except that the whole colon can be examined using a flexible tube.

CT scan CT stands for Computerized Tomography. A CT scan is an X-ray that takes computerized pictures of sections through the body. It shows up soft tissue such as tumours and not just bone as ordinary X-rays do.

DNA A cell's genetic material is made up of DNA – deoxyribonucleic acid. Alteration of the DNA can change genes and upset their function.

electron micrograph an image obtained using an electron microscope, a powerful instrument that gives extremely high magnification. Sometimes colours are put in by computer to show up particular features.

gene Each chromosome in a human cell is made of many different genes. Each gene organizes a particular function of that cell. There are many thousands of genes.

genetic mutation abnormal alteration of a cell's genetic material.

hydrocarbons chemicals that are a compound of hydrogen and carbon. They occur especially in oil, natural gas and coal.

immune system a system in the body that fights infections by producing proteins called antibodies. These attach to the infectious agent and are then destroyed by white blood cells.

immunotherapy a new form of treatment which attempts to use the patient's own immune system to fight the cancer.

incidence the frequency with which new cases of an illness occur in a population.

inherited trait something passed on from one generation to another, carried on the cell's genes; for example, eye colour.

intravenous drugs drugs given directly into the blood through a needle inserted into a vein.

leukaemia cancer of white blood cells.

lymph gland sometimes also called lymph node. These are bean-shaped glands situated along the lymphatic vessels. They filter out and destroy the toxic and infectious material in the lymphatic fluid or lymph.

lymphatic system a system of vessels that carry fluid from around cells back to the bloodstream. The function of the system is to remove and destroy toxic substances, and to resist spread of disease around the body.

lymphoma a cancer of lymph glands.

mammogram a special breast X-ray used as part of an assessment of the breast, to see if a tumour is present.

melanoma cancer of the brown-coloured or pigmented cells of the skin. It usually starts in a mole.

morphine very powerful painkiller used for severe pain in cancer care.

mortality rate the frequency with which death occurs.

palliative treatment treatment designed to improve the patient's symptoms but not aiming to cure them.

papilloma tiny cauliflower-like growth on a body surface. These can grow on skin, in the bowel, or in the genital tract.

radiotherapy cancer treatment using radiation to kill rapidly dividing cancer cells.

sigmoidoscopy a telescope examination of the 'sigmoid colon' or last part of the large bowel. The examination is performed by passing a tube through the anus into the bowel. The tube can then be looked through, to investigate the lining of the bowel.

staging an investigation of a cancer patient to assess how far advanced the disease is, in order to work out the best treatment.

survival A common way of assessing how effective a cancer treatment is is to count the number of patients who are alive 5 years after the treatment.

terminal care care of a patient during their final illness leading to their death.

thyroid gland gland in the neck that produces the hormone thyroxine. This helps to regulate the body's metabolism, for example, body temperature, heart rate, etc.

ultrasound scan a test using very high-frequency sound waves, which are directed into the body. The reflected sound is analysed by computer and an image is seen on a screen. This is very useful for investigating hollow organs in the body.

undertaker person who looks after the body after death until the funeral, and helps to organize funeral arrangements.

Resources

Cancer Research Campaign

This is a UK charity that performs pioneering cancer research. It also provides useful information about cancer, cancer treatments, etc., for patients and family.
www.crc.org.uk

Cancer Help UK

This is a free information service run by the Cancer Research Campaign.
www.cancerhelp.org.uk

Cancer BACUP

This is a UK charity providing cancer support and advice to patients and their families. Information is provided by phone, letter or email. The organization produces publications all about cancer. It also has local centres within hospitals.
Telephone: 020 7613 2121
Freephone: 0808 800 1234
www.cancerbacup.org.uk

Imperial Cancer Research Fund

This UK organization carries out research into all types of cancer. It also provides a cancer information centre.
www.imperialcancer.co.uk

The Institute of Cancer Research

This is a large UK organization carrying out cancer research. It also provides cancer information.
www.icr.ac.uk

Macmillan Cancer Relief

This UK organization provides specialist information, treatment and care for cancer patients. It has trained doctors and nurses and runs its own buildings. It provides an information line.
Telephone: 0845 601 6161
www.macmillan.org.uk

Marie Curie Cancer Care

This UK cancer-care charity runs hospices and provides nursing care to the terminally ill at home.
Telephone: 020 7599 7729
www.mariecurie.org.uk

Index